THE TOP 100 IMMUNITY BOOSTERS

THE TOP 100 IMMUNITY BOOSTERS

CHARLOTTE HAIGH

DUNCAN BAIRD PUBLISHERS

LONDON

The Top 100 Immunity Boosters
Charlotte Haigh

First published in the United Kingdom and Ireland in 2005 by
Duncan Baird Publishers Ltd
Sixth Floor
Castle House
75–76 Wells Street
London W1T 3QH

Conceived, created and designed by Duncan Baird Publishers

Managing Editor: Julia Charles
Editor: Ingrid Court-Jones
Managing Designer: Manisha Patel
Designer: Justin Ford

Library of Congress Cataloging-in-Publication Data is available

Distributed in the United States by Publishers Group West

10 9 8 7 6 5 4 3 2

ISBN-10: 1-84483-111-6   ISBN-13: 9-781844-831111

Typeset in Helvetica Condensed
Color reproduction by Scanhouse, Malaysia
Printed in Thailand by Imago

Publisher's Note: The information in this book is intended only as a guide to following a healthy diet and is not meant as a substitute for medical advice and treatment. People with special dietary requirements of any kind should consult appropriate medical professionals before changing their diet.

contents

KEY TO SYMBOLS

anti-allergenic

anti-bacterial

anti-cancer

anti-viral

anti-inflammatory

antioxidant

antiseptic

detoxifying

good for the heart

the immune system

An efficient immune system is the key to maintaining good · health. It helps to protect us from all manner of diseases from colds to cancer, fights food poisoning and keeps allergies in check, as well as slowing down the ageing process. But poor diet, an unhealthy lifestyle and a toxic environment can all compromise and weaken the immune system, leaving us prone to everything from common colds to more serious infections.

HOW IT WORKS

The immune system, which acts like a defending army, is based mainly in the lymphatic system and bloodstream, although the skin and other organs, such as the digestive system, also play an important role. The lymphatic system is a network of vessels which returns fluid from spaces between cells to the blood circulation. Lymph nodes, the spleen and the thymus gland are part of the lymph system, and they produce lymphocytes – cells which identify then set out to destroy and eliminate foreign substances, microbes and cancer cells. There are two types of lymphocytes: B-cells, and T-cells. T-cells, which are produced in the thymus, can destroy foreign bodies directly, whereas B-cells – produced in the spleen – will secrete antibodies against these undesirables in order to elimate them. Similar to lymphocytes are natural killer cells (NK) which are particularly lethal against cancer cells, destroying them outright. The white blood cells found in the bloodstream – phagocytes and lymphocytes – play an important role in immunity by destroying invading bacteria and removing dead and damaged tissue. An optimally functioning immune system is in perfect balance. So, although it is primed to destroy foreign substances, it allows entry to those that we need, such as food. For example, the gut's immune ecology contains a balance of both friendly and unfriendly bacteria. As long as the two stay in harmony, digestive immunity is strong. But if the unfriendly bacteria start to proliferate – perhaps because your diet is high in sugar and saturated fat – you can develop digestive complaints and fungal infections.

IMMUNE-SYSTEM ENEMIES

All the immune system organs and cells rely on specific nutrients to keep them working efficiently. For example, interferon, an anti-viral and anti-cancer chemical secreted by tissues throughout the body, needs vitamin C for its production, while lysozyme, an anti-bacterial enzyme found in body fluids such as tears and blood, requires vitamin A. So a poor diet will immediately result in a weakened immune system. Other enemies of strong immunity include stress, smoking, excess alcohol and caffeine, drugs (both medicinal and recreational), food additives, pesticides and pollution.

SIGNS OF LOW IMMUNITY

A poorly functioning immune system quickly makes itself known. While it's normal for most of us to have one or two colds a year, lowered immunity can make us vulnerable to every passing cold or 'flu bug, and we find ourselves succumbing to frequent infections. Other signs of inefficient immunity are digestive problems, fatigue, aching joints, muscle weakness, and poor skin.

An imbalanced immune system also causes allergies and food intolerances by launching an attack when it identifies the presence of certain trigger substances. It then releases histamine and other chemicals to drive out what it perceives as an invader, causing a plethora of unwelcome symptoms.

Autoimmunity occurs when the body goes into overdrive and starts producing antibodies which attack the body's own tissues – lupus and rheumatoid arthritis are both auto-immune diseases.

immunity-boosting foods

To keep the body's immune organs and cells healthy and in balance, it is vital to eat the right foods. The entire immune system needs vitamin C to function, so include plenty of foods rich in this antioxidant – most fruits and vegetables contain high levels of it. Vitamin A is powerfully anti-viral, and helps to maintain the thymus gland. It is found in liver, dairy foods, oily fish, cod liver oil, and in plant foods in the form of beta-carotene, which the body then converts into vitamin A. The B-vitamins are important for phagocyte (white blood cell) activity and vitamin E is a powerful antioxidant which helps stimulate antibody production.

Certain minerals are also important. Calcium helps the phagocytic cells to carry out their cleaning-up duty, while selenium is necessary for the production of antibodies. Iron builds up overall resistance, while many immune processes, including the maturation of T-cells, are heavily dependent on zinc. Most minerals can be found in seeds, nuts, and green leafy vegetables.

Protein is vital for strong immunity, as it is required to manufacture all cells, including the immune system's antibodies and enzymes. It is made up of amino acids, which play a key role in immune health – for example, the amino acid glutathione is an important antioxidant and detoxifier. Many people are deficient in protein. It is important to eat plenty of protein-rich foods such as beans, pulses, meat and fish.

Other key nutrients include fiber, which is found in whole grains, fruit, and vegetables. Fiber is vital for a healthy digestive system – it keeps the colon clear and prevents the build-up of toxins, and helps to prevent overgrowth of "bad" bacteria. Healthy poly-unsaturated fats are also important because they are high in omega-3 and -6 fatty acids, which reduce inflam-mation and boost overall immunity, so eat plenty of nuts, seeds, and oily fish.

In addition to the well-known nutrients, some foods boast particular immunity enhancing properties. Green leafy vegetables, including broccoli and cabbage, contain phytochemicals called glucosinolates, which are powerfully anti-cancerous.

Watermelon, pink grapefruit and tomatoes are rich in lycopene, another cancer-fighting champion, while berries such as strawberries and raspberries contain anti-inflammatory anthocyanins as well as ellagic acid, which can help to suppress the formation of cancer cells.

OTHER STEPS TO BOOST YOUR IMMUNITY

There are a number of other things that you can do, apart from eating a healthy diet, to boost your immunity. For example, you can take more exercise, which encourages the flow of lymph fluid containing immune cells around the body. Exercise also stimulates the circulation, improving the oxygen supply to the body's organs. You don't have to go to a gym – simply staying generally active and walking briskly for half an hour every

day will help. In fact, athletes are prone to poor health as rigorous over-exercising can actually suppress the immune system. The importance of having a positive attitude to life and a good social network cannot be overestimated – numerous studies have revealed that laughing, being optimistic, and sharing a joke with friends can boost the immune system. Getting plenty of sleep is also important, and exposure to natural daylight is key to stimulating both mood and immunity. Yoga and meditation can release stress and help you to relax.

IMMUNITY ENEMIES AT A GLANCE

- A lack of vitamins and minerals
- Sugar
- Stress
- Smoking
- Excessive intake of alcohol
- Lack of exercise
- Lack of sleep

sweet potato

This highly nutritious and delicious tuber has a unique and distinctively sweet flavor.

NUTRIENTS Vitamins B6, C, E, beta-carotene; iron, potassium; fiber

Sweet potato is a good source of vitamin C. The orange variety also contains beta-carotene (a carotenoid with anti-viral, anti-cancer and antioxidant properties) which the body converts to vitamin A – an antioxidant that helps to fight cancer. In addition, sweet potato is rich in vitamin E, which is vital for healthy skin. Full of fiber, especially the skin, this vegetable can help lower cholesterol and enhance digestive function.

SWEET POTATO SUMMER SALAD *serves 4*

3 sweet potatoes cooked in their skins, diced
4 scallions, sliced
2 sticks celery, sliced
⅔ cup walnuts, chopped
1 green bell pepper, sliced
1 cup crème fraîche
2 tbsp white wine vinegar

Place all the ingredients in a large salad bowl and mix together thoroughly. Serve as a side dish.

Always buy orange sweet potatoes – the ones with red skins – as the white variety contain far less beta-carotene.

carrot

Carrots are packed with nutrients, which are particularly beneficial for eye health and vision.

NUTRIENTS Vitamin K, beta-carotene, folate; calcium, chromium, iron, zinc; fiber

Carrots are one of the richest sources of beta-carotene, which is converted by the body into the antioxidant vitamin A. This helps to strengthen cells against viruses, to fight cancer and to prevent heart disease. It also aids vision. We use the vitamin K present in carrots for bloodclotting and the healing of wounds, while their fiber content aids digestion and keeps the heart healthy. The chromium found in carrots helps to stabilize blood sugar levels, making this vegetable useful for controlling diabetes and sugar cravings.

ZINGY CARROT JUICE
serves 2

8 carrots, scrubbed and sliced
4 green apples, sliced
1 x 2-inch piece fresh ginger

Press all the ingredients through a juicer. Serve immediately.

Raw carrots can be hard to digest, so grate or chop them finely before eating.

© ◉ ♡

yam

NUTRIENTS Vitamin B1, beta-carotene; fiber

This starchy root vegetable has been a staple food in many parts of the world for centuries.

Yams come in yellow, white and, purple varieties; the yellow one being rich in beta-carotene. This is needed by the body to produce vitamin A, which in turn is vital for strengthening cell membranes, keeping out viruses, preventing cancer, and assisting the body in dealing with pollutants. Its vitamin B1 is useful for boosting energy levels, and easing depression and stress, both of which can suppress the immune system.

YAM AND SPINACH MASH
serves 4

1lb yam, peeled and diced
4½ cups fresh spinach
3 tbsp olive oil
1 onion, sliced
kosher salt and freshly ground
   black pepper, to taste

Boil the yam until tender, then mash and set aside. Wilt the spinach in hot water. Heat the oil in a skillet and fry the onion until soft. Add the yam and the spinach, combining them well. Season with salt and pepper, and serve as a side dish.

Yams are very high in fiber and keep the digestive system in good working order.

Ⓒ Ⓞ ♡

potato

This versatile and enduringly popular vegetable can play an important role in warding off illness.

Potatoes are one of the cheapest and most readily available sources of vitamin C – a nutrient that is vital for keeping the immune system healthy. New potatoes are richer in this antioxidant than old ones. Most of the fibre, which aids digestion and lowers cholesterol, is found in the skin. Potatoes also contain vitamin B6, which helps to make the immunity-boosting amino acids that are crucial for good health. Vitamin B6 is needed by phagocytes to mop up waste matter from cells.

NUTRIENTS Vitamins B1, B3, B6, C, folate; copper, iron, potassium; fiber

GARLIC MASH
serves 4

6 medium potatoes, peeled
   and diced
5 cloves garlic
1¼ cups milk or soya
   milk
4 tbsp olive oil
1 tsp salt
1 pinch black pepper
1 tsp ground nutmeg

Boil the potatoes and garlic in the milk until tender, topping up with enough water to cover them. Add the olive oil, salt, pepper and nutmeg, then mash until smooth. Serve as a side dish.

onion

This widely eaten vegetable boosts health as well as adding depth and flavor to cooking.

NUTRIENTS Vitamins B1, B6; sulfur compounds; flavonoids

Onion has an exceptionally high level of the flavonoid quercetin, a strong antioxidant which can block the formation of cancer cells. Quercetin is anti-inflammatory, antibiotic and anti-viral and, like beta-carotene, not destroyed in cooking. Onion is also thought to suppress the activity of the *helicobacter pylori* bacterium, which causes stomach ulcers and food poisoning. It can also help to lower cholesterol, thin the blood, and prevent the formation of clots.

ONION SOUP *serves 4*

1 tbsp safflower oil
1 tbsp butter
3 large onions, finely sliced into rings
2 tsp raw cane sugar
2 tsp all-purpose flour
2¼ cups vegetable bouillon
sprig of thyme
1 tbsp soy sauce
black pepper

Melt the oil and butter in a large saucepan, then add the onion and sugar, and cook until brown. Stir in the flour and cook for 1 minute, then add the bouillon, thyme, soy sauce and black pepper. Reduce the heat and simmer for 20 minutes. Serve with cheese on toast.

Onion may cause indigestion in people with gastro-intestinal conditions, especially when eaten raw.

red bell pepper

Brightly colored bell peppers are bursting with vitamin C and beta-carotene.

Red bell peppers are one of the best sources of vitamin C, which is crucial for immune function. They also contain flavonoids that are thought to enhance vitamin C's antioxidant action by strengthening its ability to protect the body against disease. Bell peppers have high levels of beta-carotene, which the body turns into anti-viral, immunity-boosting vitamin A, and also contain fiber – important for preventing the build up of cholesterol.

Green and yellow bell peppers have similar levels of vitamin C to red ones, but less beta-carotene.

NUTRIENTS Vitamins B6, C, beta-carotene; fiber

STUFFED PEPPERS *serves 4*

3 tbsp olive oil
4 red bell peppers, topped and deseeded
½ lb cherry tomatoes
2 cloves garlic, finely chopped
1 red onion, finely chopped
1 bunch fresh basil, shredded
¾ cup mozzarella cheese, cut into small cubes
1 cup Parmesan cheese, grated
black pepper, to taste

Preheat the oven to 220°C/ 425°F/gas mark 7. Spoon 2 tbsp olive oil into a baking dish and place in the oven. Meanwhile, combine all the ingredients except the bell peppers in a bowl with 1 tbsp olive oil. Fill each pepper with equal amounts of the mixture, then put the tops on. Place in the dish and cook in the oven for 20 minutes. Serve.

007

beet

NUTRIENTS Folate; iron, manganese, potassium; betanin; fiber, protein

A useful detoxifier and blood purifier, beet is rich in a variety of nutrients crucial for immunity.

A descendant of the sea beet, which grows around the Mediterranean coast, beet has long been prized for its medicinal qualities. Traditionally, it has been used for purifying the blood. It is thought that beet was first used in Roman times and then introduced as a cooking ingredient by French chefs in the 18th century, when they began using it in dishes.

BEET'S IMMUNITY-BOOSTING PROPERTIES

Rich in iron, beet enhances the production of disease-fighting antibodies, white blood cells (including phagocytes). It also stimulates red blood cells and improves the supply of oxygen to cells. It contains manganese, which is needed for the formation of interferon, a powerful anti-cancer substance, and is given its red color by the pigment betanin, an antioxidant anthocyanin which can help prevent cancer and heart disease. Beet is thought to have detoxifying properties which improve liver and kidney health, and is high in fibre, important for both heart and digestive health.

USING BEET

As effective cooked as it is raw, fresh beet can be juiced, used in salads, or made into soup. Beet tops (leaves) are also rich in vitamin A and C, iron and calcium and can be used in a similar way to spinach. Simply boil them for a few minutes and serve warm with a little olive oil.

BEET FACTS

• Beet was prized by the ancient Greeks, who would offer it up to their gods.

• Although beet contains no potential toxins, its tops (leaves) are high in oxalic acid, so they should be avoided by anyone with arthritis or kidney stones.

• Beet has traditionally been used by herbalists as a remedy for blood ailments and it is still considered to be an effective, naturopathic treatment in modern times.

• Betanin, the pigment that produces the red coloring in beet, can turn urine pink. This may be alarming but it is harmless!

HOT BEET SOUP *serves 2*

1 onion, peeled and chopped
1 clove garlic, crushed
1 tsp chili powder
1 tbsp olive oil
1 x 14oz can tomatoes
2 fresh beets, washed
soured cream, to serve

Preheat the oven to 200°C/400°F/ gas mark 6. Wrap each beet in foil and bake for about 45 minutes until tender. Leave them to cool, then peel and dice. Sweat the garlic and onions over a low heat in the olive oil for 3 minutes.

Add the chili powder, stir together for 1 minute, add the tomatoes and bring to the boil. Simmer for 15 minutes before stirring in the beets. Pour the soup into bowls, add some soured cream, and serve.

© ● ◎

tomato

There are more than 7,000 varieties of tomato and all of them are packed full of nutrients.

Cooking tomatoes actually releases the lycopene making it more available to the body.

Tomatoes are full of vitamin C, which is powerfully anti-viral and crucial for all functions of the immune system. They are also packed with lycopene, a type of carotenoid, that helps to prevent cancer, particularly cancer of the prostate. Tomatoes contain high levels of beta-carotene – necessary for the production of vitamin A. This helps to maintain a healthy thymus gland, which plays a vital role in immune response. In addition, tomatoes are a good source of vitamin E, which helps to protect the body from toxins.

GAZPACHO *serves 4*

6 ripe tomatoes, chopped
½ onion, finely chopped
½ cucumber, peeled and diced
1 green bell pepper, diced
juice of 1 lemon
3 garlic cloves, chopped
3 tbsp fresh parsley, chopped

2 tsp vegetable bouillon
  powder

Place all the ingredients in a blender and whizz until smooth. Divide into four bowls. Chill for 30 minutes, then serve.

600

rhubarb

Used in Chinese medicine for thousands of years, this relative of dock is a powerful disease-fighter.

This sharp-tasting food contains anti-bacterial chemicals that help the body to fight off infections. It's a good source of immune-supporting vitamin C, and contains compounds which help to prevent cancer. Rhubarb is high in dietary fiber. This is helpful for lowering cholesterol and preventing heart disease, and acts as a natural laxative. It also contains oxalic acid, which is thought to aid the body to detoxify. Rhubarb should be avoided by those prone to gout and arthritis, as oxalates can worsen these conditions.

NUTRIENTS Vitamin C, folate; calcium, magnesium, potassium; fiber; oxalic acid

RHUBARB CRUMBLE
serves 4

5 stalks rhubarb, chopped
2 tbsp water
⅓ cup raw cane sugar
1¼ cups all-purpose flour
1 stick unsalted butter

Preheat the oven to 180°C/ 350°F/gas mark 4. Place the rhubarb, water and half the sugar in a saucepan and stew for 5 minutes. Meanwhile, make the topping – rub the butter into the flour until it forms the consistency of bread crumbs, then add the remaining sugar and stir. Pour the stewed rhubarb into a baking dish, spoon the crumble on top, and cook in the oven until golden. Serve.

shiitake

NUTRIENTS Vitamins B1, B2, B3, C; iron, magnesium, phosphorous, potassium; lentinan; protein

These highly-prized Japanese tree fungi have powerful disease-fighting capabilities.

Native to China, Japan, and Korea, shiitake mushrooms have been used in those countries for thousands of years to prevent and treat illness. In ancient China they were prescribed by physicians to help beat a range of conditions, from colds and 'flu to gastrointestinal problems. Recently, shiitake mushrooms have been the subject of several scientific studies that are researching their pro-immunity and healing powers.

SHIITAKE'S IMMUNITY-BOOSTING PROPERTIES

These fungi contain lentinan, a polysaccharide compound that has been shown to help lower cholesterol. Lentinan has also been isolated and licensed as an anti-cancer drug in Japan because of its ability to stimulate the immune system to deactivate malignant cells. In addition lentinan is understood to trigger the production of the anti-viral and anti-bacterial substance interferon, which may help to inhibit the progress of the virus HIV. The mushrooms are also rich in the amino acids that enhance general immune function.

Using shiitake mushroom

Shiitake mushrooms are more expensive than many varieties, but a small amount gives health benefits and satisfies apetite. They can be bought fresh, pickled or dried, and can be used in dishes in the same way as ordinary field mushrooms.

SHIITAKE FACTS

• In ancient China, shiitake mushrooms were prized so highly that they were reserved for consumption by the emperor and his family.

• Shiitake is one of a number of medicinal mushrooms which, more than any other food, are currently being studied for their potent pro-immunity properties. Other well researched fungi are maitake and reishi.

• The health-boosting benefits of shiitake are now available in supplement form but as they have anti-bloodclotting properties those on blood thinning medication should avoid excessive amounts.

SHIITAKE NOODLES *serves 4*

9oz thick egg noodles
3 tbsp soy sauce
1 tbsp oyster sauce
1 tsp brown sugar
1 tbsp sesame oil
2 small red chilies, sliced and
   deseeded
1 package firm tofu, diced
1 x 2-inch piece fresh ginger,

grated
2 cloves garlic, crushed
2½ cups fresh shiitake
   mushrooms, sliced
6 scallions, chopped

Cover the noodles in boiling water and leave to soften for 5 minutes. Drain. In a bowl, mix together

the soy sauce, oyster sauce and sugar. Heat the oil in a wok. Stir-fry the chilies, tofu, ginger and garlic for 2 minutes, then add the noodles, mushrooms, sauce mixture, and scallions. Toss and serve immediately.

© ◎

pumpkin

NUTRIENTS Vitamin C, beta-carotene; fiber

The most famous of all the winter squashes has flesh crammed with cancer-fighting chemicals.

Orange-fleshed pumpkins contain high levels of carotenoids, which studies suggest may help to prevent some forms of cancer, including cancer of the colon, as well as heart disease. Pumpkins are also rich in antioxidant vitamin C, which is needed for efficient immune system function, and can help to fight viruses such as colds, as well as improve general overall resistance to disease. In addition, pumpkins contain fiber, which helps lower cholesterol, and promotes good digestion by encouraging the elimination of waste.

Choose orange pumpkins as they contain the highest amount of carotenoids.

PUMPKIN FRITTERS *serves 2*

1 medium pumpkin, cut into
thick slices
1⅓ cups plain wholewheat
flour
½ tsp salt
½ tsp baking powder
2 tsp ground cumin
yolk and white of 1 egg
¾ cup water
1 onion, chopped

2 garlic cloves, crushed
2 tbsp olive oil

Steam the pumpkin for 10 minutes, then leave to cool. In a bowl, combine the flour, salt, baking powder, and cumin, then add the egg yolk and the water, a little at a time, stirring to form a smooth paste.

Add the onion and garlic, then whisk the egg white and fold it in to the mixture. Heat the oil in a skillet, then dip the pumpkin slices in the mixture and fry a few at a time, turning regularly, until crisp and brown. Serve warm.

chili pepper

Fiery chilies make effective natural painkillers.

Even in small amounts, chilies are a helpful addition to the diet – one small red chili contains high levels of the anti-viral, anti-cancer and antioxidant carotenoid beta-carotene, some of which is converted into vitamin A in the body. Both these nutrients help to prevent the damage caused by toxins in the body, and can help stave off cancer and premature ageing. Chilies also contain capsaicin, a plant chemical that has natural analgesic properties, which can be used both internally and topically to ease headaches, arthritis, and sinusitis.

NUTRIENTS Vitamin C, beta-carotene; capsaicin; fiber

SPICY RICE *serves 2*

1 cup long-grain rice
zest of 1 lime
1 clove garlic, peeled
1 red chili, sliced
zest and juice of 2 lemons
1 tbsp wholegrain mustard
4 tbsp olive oil

Add the rice, lime zest and garlic to a saucepan, cover with water, bring to a boil, and simmer until the rice is tender. Drain and remove the lime zest and garlic. Combine the remaining ingredients in a bowl, then stir the mixture into the rice. Serve as a side dish.

Chilies have mild mood-boosting properties.

avocado

NUTRIENTS Vitamins B1, B2, B3, B5, E, K, biotin, carotenoids, folate; potassium, zinc; beta-sitosterol, glutathione; omega-6 fatty acids; fiber

One of the few fruits that contains fat, avocado boasts a wealth of health-boosting properties.

Strictly speaking, avocado is a fruit, although it is typically used in savory dishes. It is native to Central America, and was discovered by Spanish invaders in the 16th century. It is now popular throughout the world and grown in various tropical regions. With a smooth, buttery texture and mild, creamy taste, avocado is best eaten when ripe.

AVOCADO'S IMMUNITY-BOOSTING PROPERTIES

Avocados contains monounsaturated fat which can help lower cholesterol. In addition, they are a source of linoleic acid (also known as omega-6 fatty acid), which the body converts to gamma-linolenic acid (GLA), a substance that helps to thin the blood, soothe inflammation and improve blood-sugar balance. They are rich in vitamin E, an antioxidant that neutralizes the damaging effect of toxins in the body and boosts resistance to infection. Avocado's B-vitamin levels help the immune cells to destroy harmful invaders – as does glutathione, a powerful substance that boosts the action of the body's natural killer cells. Last but not least, they contain the plant chemical beta-sitosterol which is particularly beneficial to the prostate gland.

USING AVOCADO

Avocados are normally picked before they are ripe, and take about a week to ripen at room temperature, although storing them in a paper bag with a banana can speed the process.

AVOCADO FACTS

• The avocado has been known by several names, including alligator pear and butter pear. It earned the title butter pear because of its smooth texture, but alligator pear was the original name given to it by the Spanish.

• Stop opened avocados from turning brown by sprinkling the exposed surfaces with lemon juice and leaving the stone in.

• Avocado is also an effective skin treatment – simply mash the flesh and smooth it over your face, washing off after 10 minutes.

• People with latex allergies are also likely to be allergic to avocado.

GUACAMOLE *makes 1 large bowl*

2 ripe avocados, peeled and pitted
juice of 1 lime
2 cloves garlic, crushed
1 medium onion, finely chopped
2 tomatoes, peeled and chopped

1 small red chili, deseeded and finely chopped
1 tbsp fresh cilantro, finely chopped

For a chunky dip, mash the avocados by hand with the lime

juice until smooth, then add the remaining ingredients and combine thoroughly. For a smoother texture blend the ingredients in a food processor Serve as a dip for crudités.

014

spinach

This versatile leafy vegetable is popular worldwide and has powerful anti-carcinogenic properties.

NUTRIENTS Vitamins B2, B3, C, E, carotenoids, folate; calcium, magnesium, zinc; fiber

Spinach is rich in carotenoids, which the body converts to antioxidant vitamin A to help to trigger immune response to fight infections. This vegetable helps to prevent lung, breast, and cervical cancers, as well as to fight heart disease. Its vitamin C content keeps skin and mucous membranes healthy, while its B vitamins improve energy and nervous-system conditions. Spinach is also rich in zinc, required to promote T-cell activity.

SPINACH RISOTTO *serves 4*

1 tbsp olive oil
½ stick unsalted butter
2 onions, finely chopped
1¼ cups Arborio rice
1 small glass white wine
3¾ cups vegetable stock
4 good handfuls fresh
  spinach, washed
1 cup Parmesan
  cheese, grated

Heat the oil and butter in a pan, and lightly fry the onions until golden. Add the rice, stirring for 1 minute, then add the wine and heat until absorbed. Add enough stock to cover, leave to absorb, then keep adding stock until all of it is used and the rice is cooked. Stir in the spinach and cook until slightly wilted. Remove from heat and sprinkle with cheese. Serve.

Spinach is best eaten raw or lightly cooked as heavy cooking removes its carotenoids and vitamin C.

asparagus

This delicate and luxurious spring vegetable is a surprisingly potent force in the fight for health.

NUTRIENTS Vitamins B3, C, beta-carotene, folate; potassium, zinc; asparagin; flavonoids; fiber

Asparagus is a natural diuretic, encouraging the body to flush out toxins. Its cleansing, anti-inflammatory properties make it useful for easing indigestion, irritable bowel syndrome, and rheumatoid arthritis. Asparagus is a good source of folate, beta-carotene, vitamin C, and the antioxidant glutathione, which can all lower the risk of heart disease and cancer. It is also rich in the flavonoid rutin, which we need to maintain a healthy circulation and asparagin, a detoxifying amino acid.

The most tender part of the asparagus plant is the tip, so steam it gently to preserve the vitamin content.

BAKED ASPARAGUS TIPS
serves 4

1 bunch asparagus tips
2 tbsp olive oil
kosher salt and black pepper, to taste
Parmesan shavings, to serve

Spread the asparagus flat on a baking sheet, and drizzle the olive oil over it. Season with the salt and pepper. Bake in the oven on a low heat for 15 minutes, until the asparagus is tender. Sprinkle over the Parmesan shavings, and serve.

NUTRIENTS Vitamins B3, B5, biotin, folate; potassium, zinc; cynarin

globe artichoke

This attractive and sophisticated vegetable is a form of thistle and a member of the daisy family.

Globe artichoke has traditionally been used as a hangover remedy because it contains cynarin, a compound that supports the liver. This substance also gives artichoke its detoxifying qualities, and it is said to ease the symptoms of irritable bowel syndrome. Its high levels of B-vitamins are beneficial for boosting energy and mental alertness, and play an important role in strengthening the immune-system.

ARTICHOKE SALAD

serves 4

8 artichoke hearts
4 large tomatoes, cut into wedges
1 red onion, finely sliced
½ green bell pepper, chopped
½ cup green olives
1 clove garlic, crushed
6 tbsp olive oil
4 tbsp lemon juice
1 tsp Dijon mustard
kosher salt and pepper

If using fresh artichokes, break off the outer leaves and cut away the inner leaves. Scrape out the choke and boil the heart for about 20 minutes until tender. Rinse under cold water and combine in a large bowl with the tomatoes, onion, green pepper and olives. Whisk the remaining ingredients to make the dressing, drizzle over the vegetables and serve.

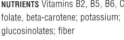

Brussels sprouts

This relative of the cabbage is an effective cancer-fighter thanks to its high levels of antioxidants.

NUTRIENTS Vitamins B2, B5, B6, C, folate, beta-carotene; potassium; glucosinolates; fiber

Brussels sprouts are one of the best sources of glucosinolates, which help the body to produce cancer-preventing enzymes. They are also high in vitamin C and folate, which encourage the body to heal itself. Brussels sprouts contain vitamin B5, an immune stimulant that triggers the production of antibodies. Dense in fiber, Brussels sprouts keep the digestive system healthy and cholesterol low.

> Brussels sprouts are named after the capital of Belgium, where they were first grown in the 16th century.

NUTTY SPROUT STIR-FRY *serves 4*

2 onions, peeled and sliced
1 cup blanched
  almonds, lightly toasted
4 tbsp olive oil
1¼ lb Brussels
  sprouts, peeled and sliced
black pepper, to taste

Gently fry the onions and almonds in the oil until the onions are soft. Blanch the sprouts for 1 minute in a saucepan of lightly salted boiling water, then add to the pan with the onions and almonds, cooking gently until the sprouts are soft. Season to taste with black pepper and serve.

Ⓒ Ⓞ ⬧ ♡

nettle

NUTRIENTS Vitamins B1, B2, B3, B5, C, K, beta-carotene; calcium, iron, magnesium, potassium

Not just a stinging weed, nettle is packed with health-boosting minerals and vitamins.

Nettle makes an excellent cleanser; its diuretic properties help to rid the body of waste products linked with conditions such as gout, acne, and arthritis. High in many nutrients, it fortifies the immune system and is therefore useful to help ease chronic disease and for aiding recovery from illness. Its antioxidant content makes nettle an effective cancer-fighter.

NETTLE AND LEMON TEA
makes 1 cup

2 fresh nettle tips
1 thick wedge of lemon
1 cup boiling water

Wash the nettle tips (wearing plastic gloves) and place them in a tea strainer in a mug. Pour on the boiling water and add the lemon. Let infuse for 5 minutes, and drink when cool.

Always cook nettle before eating it, and wear gloves to handle the fresh plant.

watercress

This robustly-flavored salad leaf is a powerful immune system stimulant.

Watercress is rich in glucosinolates – plant chemicals that boost the activity of cancer-preventing enzymes. It contains the key antioxidant vitamins needed for a fully-functioning immune system, along with vitamin B6, which enhances the action of phagocytes – white blood cells responsible for cleaning up waste matter. Watercress is also a good source of the mineral manganese, and iron, which can both help the body to resist infections.

Traditionally watercress has been used to boost the metabolism and detoxify the body.

NUTRIENTS Vitamins B3, B6, C, E, K, beta-carotene (and other carotenoids); calcium, manganese, iron, zinc; glucosinolates; fiber

WATERCRESS DIP
makes 1 bowl

a large handful of watercress leaves, chopped
1 onion, chopped
1 ripe avocado, peeled, pitted and sliced
juice of ½ a lemon
pinch of vegetable bouillon powder
1 clove garlic

Place all the ingredients together in a blender and process until smooth. Serve as a dip for crudités.

Belgian endive

NUTRIENTS Vitamins B1, folate, beta-carotene; iron, phosphorous; fiber

A good digestive stimulant, endive was originally grown for its root which was added to coffee.

Belgian endive (also known as chicory) contains bitters, which help to stimulate the digestive system and detoxify the liver. It is also rich in beta-carotene, which is converted by the body into vitamin A – an antioxidant that helps to prevent cancer and has potent anti-viral properties. It also contains vitamin B1, an important energy-booster that keeps mucous membranes and nerves healthy. Belgian endive is a good source of fiber, helping to regulate the elimination of waste from the body, and lowering cholesterol levels.

BRAISED ENDIVE *serves 2–3*

2 Belgian endives, sliced
1 small red apple, diced
2 tbsp fresh lemon juice
2 tsp olive oil
kosher salt and black pepper, to taste
1 tbsp fresh parsley, chopped
2 tbsp white wine vinegar
water to cover

Place all the ingredients, apart from the vinegar and the parsley, in a large saucepan and cook on a low heat until the water evaporates. Drain, and sprinkle with the vinegar and the parsley. Serve as a side dish.

cauliflower

Thought to have originated from China, cauliflower is a good source of phytochemicals.

NUTRIENTS Vitamins B3, B5, B6, C, folate; calcium, potassium, zinc; glucosinolates; fiber

Like other members of the *Cruciferous* family, cauliflower contains glucosinolates, plant chemicals that can help prevent cancer, especially of the lung, breast, stomach, and colon. It also contains vitamin C and zinc, which are both crucial for strengthening the immune system. Cauliflower is a good source of B-vitamins, including folate, which is vital for good reproductive health, and B5, needed for antibody production.

Cauliflower has anti-allergenic properties that can help to ease asthma and skin allergies.

INDIAN–STYLE CAULIFLOWER *serves 4*

1 onion, finely chopped	In a skillet gently fry
1 tbsp olive oil	the onion in the oil for 5
1 clove garlic, crushed	minutes. Add the garlic, spices,
1 tsp ground ginger	cauliflower, and water. Cover
1 tsp ground coriander	and simmer, stirring
1 tsp turmeric	occasionally until the cauliflower
1 medium cauliflower, cut into	is tender. Continue to cook,
small florets	stirring, until the cauliflower is
2 tbsp water	dry. Serve as a side dish.

curly kale

NUTRIENTS Vitamins B2, B3, B6, C, E, K, beta-carotene, folate; calcium, iron, magnesium, zinc; flavonoids, glucosinolates, fiber

Bursting with vitamins and phytochemicals, kale is an important immunity-booster.

Curly kale is thought to have originated in the Mediterranean region. Like cabbage and Brussels sprouts, it is a member of the *Cruciferous* family, sharing with these vegetables the ability to retain high levels of water and nutrients in its leaves, which makes it a highly beneficial food.

CURLY KALE'S IMMUNITY-BOOSTING PROPERTIES

Kale contains high levels of glucosinolates, natural plant chemicals which block cancer-causing substances, stimulate detoxifying and repair enzymes in the body and suppress cancer cell division. It also contains flavonoids, which are needed for healthy circulation and to stimulate immune response, and plant sterols, important for keeping cholesterol levels low. In addition, curly kale is packed with B-vitamins that improve energy and bolster the immune system's ability to mop up invader cells. It has high levels of antioxidant vitamin C and beta-carotene. It also contains vitamin K, which promotes blood clotting and healing, and good amounts of immunity-boosting minerals, including iron and zinc.

USING CURLY KALE

Curly kale can be eaten raw, steamed and served as a side dish, or lightly stir-fried. Kale is in season in winter, and is a nutritious addition to the diet during the colder months.

CURLY KALE FACTS

• Curly kale, like other members of the *Cruciferous* family is thought to have hormone-balancing properties that help to prevent breast and ovarian cancer.

• Vegetables in the *Cruciferous* family are possibly the most important plant foods with regard to cancer prevention, because of their high glucosinolate content.

• In some parts of Europe, curly kale is known as *borecole*, derived from a Dutch word meaning "peasants' cabbage".

• The nutrients in curly kale are particularly beneficial to the skin and encourage wound healing and maintainance of healthy cell membranes.

TENDER PARSLEY KALE *serves 4*

2¼ lb curly kale	Wash and shred the kale leaves.
2 tbsp olive oil	Heat the oil in a large saucepan,
kosher salt and black pepper,	add the kale, cover and cook on
to taste	a low heat until the leaves are
3 tbsp fresh parsley, chopped	tender. Season with salt and
½ tsp ground nutmeg	pepper, stir the parsley and
	nutmeg through for 1 minute,
	then serve immediately.

 broccoli

NUTRIENTS Vitamins B3, B5, C, E, folate, beta-carotene; calcium, iron, zinc; sulforaphanes

One of the best weapons against disease, broccoli packs a more powerful nutrient punch than any other vegetable.

Broccoli is a powerhouse of antioxidant vitamin C, which is crucial for immune response. It is also a rich source of carotenoids, which are important for the thymus gland that regulates the immune system, and is packed with B-vitamins, needed for good immune and nervous system health. Broccoli contains sulforaphanes, powerful anti-carcinogenic chemicals that fight the development of tumors. It's also full of fiber, vital for a healthy digestive system, and has detoxifying properties to help cleanse the liver.

Aim for two or three servings of broccoli a week to help prevent cancer, heart disease, and colds.

BROCCOLI STIR-FRY *serves 2*

2 tbsp sesame oil
1 x 2-inch piece fresh ginger, grated
1 head of broccoli, washed and chopped
1 clove of garlic, crushed

Heat the oil gently, then add the ginger and broccoli. Stir-fry for 3 minutes, before adding the garlic. Contine to cook for another 2 minutes. Serve immediately, as a side dish.

© ⊜ ♡

savoy cabbage

This tender leaf is a powerful detoxifier.

Savoy cabbage contains antioxidant vitamin C, needed for good overall immune function, and beta-carotene, which is converted into cancer-preventing vitamin A in the body. It is also a good source of vitamin B3 – needed for energy, and healthy muscles and nerves – and folate, a key substance for good reproductive health. Savoy cabbage contains glucosinolates, plant chemicals containing powerful enzymes that research suggests help to protect against cancer.

NUTRIENTS Vitamins B3, C, folate, beta-carotene; calcium, iron, potassium; glucosinolates; fiber

SWEET SAVOY CABBAGE
serves 4

3 tbsp olive oil
1 tbsp mustard seeds
1 Savoy cabbage, shredded
2 cloves garlic, crushed
2 tbsp shredded coconut
1 tbsp maple syrup
2 tbsp lemon juice
kosher salt and black pepper
  to taste

Heat the oil in a wok, add the mustard seeds and stir-fry until they pop. Add the cabbage and garlic and fry until the leaves wilt, then add the coconut, maple syrup and lemon juice. Stir-fry for 1 minute, and season. Serve as a side dish.

Savoy cabbage is rich in iron, which helps to boost the transport of oxygen around the bloodstream.

C O O ⬙

arugula

NUTRIENTS Vitamin C, beta-carotene; volatile oils; fiber; sulforaphane

This hot, peppery salad leaf is packed with essential disease-fighting nutrients.

Arugula contains high levels of vitamin C, a powerfully antioxidant nutrient that helps to prevent the body against toxins and boosts resistance to viruses and other infections. It is also rich in beta-carotene, which the body uses to make cancer-fighting vitamin A. Arugula also contains high concentrations of sulforaphane, a substance shown to have potent anti-cancer properties, and it is a good source of fiber.

ARUGULA AND STEAK OPEN SANDWICHES serves 4

4 slices wholegrain bread
1¼ sticks butter
2 tbsp fresh parsley, chopped
4 minute steaks
2 large tomatoes, sliced
a large handful of arugula leaves, washed

Lightly broil the bread on both sides. Mix together the butter and parsley, and spread over the toast. Broil the steaks for 1 minute on each side, then place them on top of the toast slices. Top with the tomatoes and arugula leaves and serve.

Arugula can be cooked lightly, but it is more frequently used raw, as a salad vegetable.

kiwi fruit

Containing more vitamin C than oranges, kiwi fruit is a top immunity booster.

Kiwi fruit's immunity-enhancing abilities lie mainly in its super-dose of vitamin C. Just one fruit contains around 120 per cent of an adult's daily recommended intake, and unlike many other fruits, the nutrients remain intact long after harvesting, with 90 per cent of its vitamin C content still present after 6 months' storage. Kiwi fruit is also a good source of fiber, which we need for an efficient digestive system and a healthy heart.

NUTRIENTS Vitamins B3, C, beta-carotene; fiber

Kiwi fruit can cause allergic reactions in some children.

TROPICAL FRUIT SALAD
serves 4

4 kiwi fruits, peeled and sliced
1 mango, peeled, pitted and cubed
1 papaya, peeled, deseeded and sliced
8 lychees, peeled, pitted and halved
1 pineapple, peeled and cubed
pulp of 4 passion fruits

Combine all of the prepared fruit in a large bowl. Leave for an hour for the juices to mingle, then serve.

C ✋ ○ ♥

pineapple

NUTRIENTS Vitamins B1, B2, C; manganese; bromelain, fiber

Pineapple is rich in the enzyme bromelain, which helps to reduce inflammation and swelling.

Fresh pineapple contains bromelain – a protein-digesting enzyme that aids the digestive system and inhibits the action of a number of inflammatory agents, thereby easing inflammatory conditions, such as sinusitis, rheumatoid arthritis and gout, and speeding recovery from injuries and surgery. Pineapple is also an excellent source of manganese – an essential co-factor in a number of enzymes important for antioxidant defences and energy production. In addition, pineapple is rich in vitamin C, which supports the immune system and defends against free radicals.

PINEAPPLE AND CUCUMBER SALAD *serves 2*

1 large cucumber, peeled and
   thinly sliced
2 cups fresh pineapple, peeled,
   cored and chopped
2 tbsp mayonnaise mixed with
   lemon juice
fresh mint leaves, to garnish

Put the cucumber in a colander, sprinkle with salt and leave for 4 minutes. Rinse away the salt and squeeze out the water. In a bowl, mix the cucumber and pineapple. Chill for 2 hours, then toss in the mayonnaise. Garnish with mint leaves to serve.

C ✋ ◎ ♡

papaya

Also known as paw paw, this tropical fruit has sweet flesh rich in carotenoids and antioxidants.

Papaya is an excellent source of vitamin C and beta-carotene. As well as supporting the immune system, these antioxidants prevent the build-up of plaque on blood vessel walls, protecting against cardiovascular disease. Papaya is also rich in fiber, which lowers cholesterol levels and helps to prevent colon cancer by binding with cancer-causing toxins. In addition, it contains a protein-digesting enzyme called papain, which aids digestion and reduces inflammation.

NUTRIENTS Vitamins C, carotenoids, folate; potassium; papain, fiber

BAKED PAPAYA WITH GINGER *serves 2*

3 papayas, halved and
 deseeded
½ stick unsalted butter
5 chunks of preserved ginger,
 chopped
juice and zest of 1 lime
1 tbsp of preserved ginger
 syrup

Preheat the oven to 180°C/ 350°F/gas mark 4. Place the papayas in an oiled baking dish. Blend the butter and chopped ginger with half the lime juice and zest. Pour the mixture into the papayas. Sprinkle with the remaining lime juice, and zest followed by the ginger syrup. Bake until tender. Serve topped with plain bio-yoghurt, if desired.

apricot

NUTRIENTS Vitamins B2, B3, B5, C; beta-carotene; calcium, iron, zinc; fiber

These fragrant stone fruits are bursting with nutrients, and are delicious eaten fresh or dried.

High in fiber, apricots encourage detoxification, speeding up the body's elimination of waste matter. They are rich in beta-carotene, which is needed to form cancer-protective vitamin A, and they contain vitamin B5, which is crucial for the production of antibodies. They are also a good source of vitamin C – essential for all immune functions. In addition, dried apricots are excellent providers of resistance-boosting iron.

APRICOT CRUMBLE
serves 4

**2lb fresh apricots,
    peeled, halved and stoned**
⅓ cup raw cane sugar
⅔ cup wholewheat flour
¼ cup oats
2 tbsp light brown sugar
**½ stick unsalted butter, cut
    into small pieces**

Preheat the oven to 190°C/ 375°F/gas mark 5. Roughly chop the apricots and place them in a baking dish. Sprinkle over the raw cane sugar. In another bowl, combine the remaining ingredients and rub together until mixture resembles bread crumbs. Cover the apricots with the crumble and cook for 40 minutes. Serve with crème fraîche if desired.

Avoid bright orange dried apricots, as they have been treated with sulfur.

030

Ⓒ ◉ Ⓞ ⬦

guava

This highly-scented tropical treat is exceptionally high in vitamin C, and an effective detoxifier.

Guava gets its deep orange color from beta-carotene, which the body turns into vitamin A. Important for keeping viruses at bay and helping to prevent cancer, vitamin A is a powerful antioxidant that works with vitamin C to mop up damaging free radicals and keep the body's organs healthy. Guava is rich in fiber and has detoxifying properties. In addition it can help to calm autoimmune disorders, such as rheumatoid arthritis.

NUTRIENTS Vitamins B3, C, beta-carotene; fiber

GUAVA CRUSH

1 guava, peeled and diced
1 small orange, peeled and segmented
2 green apples, diced
1 slice lime, to decorate

Press the ingredients through a juicer. Serve with ice and garnished with a slice of lime.

Guava acts as an immune system stimulant, helping to trigger immune response.

Cantaloupe melon

NUTRIENTS Vitamins B3, C, beta-carotene

This summer melon takes its name from the town of Cantaloupe near Rome.

Cantaloupe melon is one of the richest sources of beta-carotene, which the body converts to vitamin A, an antioxidant that is crucial for the production of disease-fighting lymphocyte cells. This fruit is also rich in vitamin C, which we need for all immune functions and to protect us against colds, cancer, and heart disease. Its high water content gives it a mildly diuretic action, helping to detoxify the body.

RED MELON SALAD

serves 4

2 Cantaloupe melons, peeled, deseeded and cubed
1 pink grapefruit, divided into segments
10 raspberries
1 x 2-inch piece fresh ginger, grated

Combine the melon and grapefruit pieces in a large bowl and leave for 30 minutes to allow the juices to mingle. Divide into 4 serving bowls and garnish with the raspberries and the ginger.

passion fruit

Dense with vitamins, this intensely fragrant fruit with edible seeds is an effective energy booster.

NUTRIENTS Vitamins B2, B3, C, beta-carotene; iron, magnesium, phosphorus, zinc; fiber

Passion fruit is a good source of vitamin C, which fights viruses and bacteria. It also contains carotenoids, which the body transforms into antioxidant vitamin A, an important cancer-fighter, while its B-vitamins help keep the muscles and nervous system healthy and maintain steady energy levels. In addition, passion fruit contains fiber, which is important for a healthy digestive system and heart.

Passion fruit contains substances which can help to ease depression and anxiety.

PASSION FRUIT SORBET *serves 4*

½ cup water
⅔ cup raw cane sugar
1¾ cups passion fruit, blended to a pulp

Place the water and sugar in a large saucepan and gently heat, stirring until the sugar

dissolves. Bring to a boil, then reduce heat and simmer for 1 minute. Remove from the heat and let cool. When cool, mix in the passion fruit. Place in a plastic container and freeze until solid. Stir before serving.

C O ⇔ ♡

banana

NUTRIENTS Vitamins B3, B5, B6, C, biotin; magnesium, manganese, potassium; fiber

The best-known tropical fruit contains "moderate-releasing" sugars that provide an energy boost.

Bananas contain high levels of B-vitamins, which the body needs to produce energy. These include vitamin B5, which aids the formation of the immune system's killer cells, and B6, which improves the body's ability to clear away waste matter. Bananas are also a good source of immunity-enhancing vitamin C, and contain manganese, which works with this vitamin to produce the virus-fighting substance interferon. In addition, they are dense in fiber, and potassium, which regulates body fluids and nerve function.

BROILED BANANAS WITH LIME SYRUP *serves 2*

½ cup raw cane sugar
juice and zest of 2 limes
½ cup water
4 bananas, sliced into chunks

Put half the sugar in a saucepan with the lime juice and zest, and the water. Bring to a boil, reduce the heat and simmer for 10 minutes until thick. Place the bananas on some foil, sprinkle with the remaining sugar, and broil, turning occasionally, until golden and soft. Drizzle with the syrup, and serve.

grape

These sweet and juicy vine fruits are nature's cleansers and make excellent detoxifiers.

NUTRIENTS Vitamins B3, B6, biotin; potassium, selenium, zinc; anthocyanins, ellagic acid

Grapes are rich in antioxidant anthocyanins, which help to strengthen capillaries, so they are an excellent food for helping to improve circulation and heart health. Their high antioxidant content means that they are helpful for mopping up harmful free radicals, making them powerful detoxifiers of the skin, liver, kidneys, and bowels. Grapes can help to stabilize immune response by moderating allergic reactions. They also contain cancer-preventing ellagic acid.

Red grapes contain much higher levels of anthocyanins than white ones.

GRAPE CLEANSER *serves 1–2*

20 seedless grapes
6 stalks of celery
handful of watercress

Press the ingredients through a juicer, alternating the grapes, celery, and watercress. Mix well, and drink immediately.

apple

NUTRIENTS Vitamin C; malic acid, flavonoids; fiber

The apple is an effective cleaning tool, rich in fiber that helps clear toxins from the body.

Apples have a cleansing effect on the body, largely because they contain a form of fiber called pectin, which binds with cholesterol, toxins and heavy metals, speeding their excretion. The flavonoid quercetin found in apples is anti-inflammatory and can help to ease allergic reactions and inflammatory conditions such as arthritis, while their malic acid content helps the body to use energy efficiently. Studies have found that eating apples can also help improve lung function.

BAKED APPLES *serves 2*

½ stick unsalted butter
4 tsp dried currants
4 tsp raw cane sugar
4 tsp flaked almonds
1 tsp ground cinnamon
1 tsp ground nutmeg
2 large tart apples, peeled and cored
2 tbsp natural fromage frais, to serve

Preheat the oven to 180°C/350°F/ gas mark 4. Combine all the ingredients, apart from the apples, in a bowl. Divide the mixture in half and stuff into each apple. Wrap the apples individually in foil, and bake for 20 minutes. Serve topped with the fromage frais.

mango

Regarded by many as the most delicious tropical fruit, mango is also crammed full of nutrients.

Mango is an excellent source of beta-carotene, the precursor to anti-viral vitamin A. It also contains high levels of vitamin C, which is crucial for good overall immune function. This increasingly popular exotic fruit is one of the few fruit sources of vitamin E, an important antioxidant which helps to fight damaging free radicals in the body, as well as boosting the action of disease-battling antibodies.

NUTRIENTS Vitamins B3, C, E, beta-carotene; fiber

Mango is perfect in fruit salads and desserts, but it works equally well in savory dishes.

MANGO SMOOTHIE
serves 2

1 mango, peeled, pitted and sliced
½ fresh pineapple, peeled, cored and chopped
10 strawberries, hulled
1 cup pineapple juice
1 cup plain bio-yoghurt

Place all the ingredients in a blender and whizz until smooth and creamy. Serve immediately.

037

© ⊙ ✿

lemon

NUTRIENTS Vitamin C, folate; potassium; limonene; fibre

Arguably the most useful of all fruits, the lemon contains a wealth of health-enhancing properties.

Squeezing lemon juice onto peeled fruit, such as apples and bananas stops them from turning brown.

Like other citrus fruits, lemon is a powerhouse of antioxidant vitamin C, which helps to boost the immune system and is vital for healthy skin and gums. It contains limonene, a chemical which has been shown to slow the rate of cancer growth, and has antiseptic qualities to help kill germs – one of the reasons it is traditionally used as a gargle for sore throats. Lemon also has antifungal properties.

ZESTY LEMON DRESSING

¼ cup lemon juice
¾ cup freshly pressed
   tomato juice
1 clove garlic , crushed
1 tsp wholegrain mustard
zest of 1 lemon, finely
   shredded

Add all the ingredients, apart from the lemon zest, to a jar with a screw top and shake well. Pour into a bowl and add the zest, blending in with a fork. Drizzle immediately over a salad.

orange

This popular and versatile citrus fruit is bursting with immunity-boosting vitamins.

Oranges are one of the top sources of vitamin C, which is crucial for strong immunity, helping to fight viruses, produce disease-fighting cells, and battle bacteria. They also contain beta-sitosterol, a plant sterol that has been shown to help prevent tumor formation and to lower blood cholesterol. In addition, oranges also contain vitamin B5, which helps to stimulate immune response, and are high in the fiber needed for a healthy heart and digestive system.

NUTRIENTS Vitamins B3, B5, C, carotenoids, folate; beta-sitosterol, potassium; fiber

TANGY PANCAKES
serves 4

1 egg
⅔ cup skimmed milk
½ cup all-purpose flour
2 oranges
a knob of unsalted butter
1 tbsp raw cane sugar
4 tbsp plain bio-yoghurt

Beat together the egg and milk, then fold in the flour and grated zest of one orange. Peel both the oranges, and divide them into segments. Put these in a saucepan. Add the sugar, and cook over a low heat for 2 minutes. Melt a little butter in a skillet, then add a quarter of the batter mixture for each pancake, cooking until golden brown, turning once. Serve with the oranges and the plain bio-yoghurt.

grapefruit

NUTRIENTS Vitamin C, beta-carotene, folate; potassium; lycopene; flavonoids; fiber

This sharp and tangy breakfast fruit is detoxifying and immune-strengthening.

The grapefruit is thought to have originated in the West Indies before reaching the rest of the world in the 18th century. There are several different varieties, including sour-tasting yellow ones, and the sweeter pink, and ruby red types.

GRAPEFRUIT'S IMMUNITY-BOOSTING PROPERTIES

Every part of a grapefruit is a powerful detoxifier. Its high vitamin C content enhances immunity and tissue growth, and the flesh and rind are thought to contain compounds that help inhibit cancer development. The pulp is high in pectin, a soluble fiber that binds with excess cholesterol to remove it from the body, and helps to eliminate toxins and waste, relieving constipation. Its seeds contain an anti-parasitic, anti-fungal compound which, although not edible whole, can be taken in supplement form (grapefruit seed extract).

USING GRAPEFRUIT

The sweet pink variety, which is richer in beta-carotene, is the best option for those who dislike bitter flavors. Grapefruit is delicious eaten on its own, cut in half so that the flesh can be scooped out. It also works well juiced, either alone or in combination with other fruit, such as apple or raspberries, although juicing removes the fiber content.

GRAPEFRUIT FACTS

• Grapefruit juice can enhance the action of certain prescribed drugs, including some sleeping pills, so check with your doctor if you are taking medication.

• The white pith that lines the skin and divides the segments is thought to be particularly rich in pectin, so eat this to gain the full benefits for your heart.

• The scent of grapefruit has been found to suppress the appetite and lift the mood – try adding a couple of drops of grapefruit essential oil to a tissue and sniffing it.

STUFFED GRAPEFRUIT *serves 4*

2 grapefruits, halved, flesh removed and chopped	1 green bell pepper, deseeded and chopped	Mix the grapefruit flesh with the avocado, ginger, pear, and green bell pepper, and divide the filling among the 4 halves. Garnish with the olives and lemon balm, and serve.
1 avocado, peeled, pitted and cubed	2 black olives, pitted and halved	
1 x 1-inch piece fresh ginger, chopped	2 tbsp fresh lemon balm, finely chopped	
1 pear, peeled, cored and cubed		

lime

NUTRIENTS Vitamin C, folate; calcium, potassium; fiber

High in vitamin C, the tangy flesh of lime is an effective immune stimulant.

Lime has high levels of immune-essential vitamin C. It has powerful anti-viral properties and triggers the production of phagocytes, which mop up the invaders that cause disease, as well as fighting bacteria. The vitamin C content keeps the immune system balanced and soothes allergic reactions. Lime is also a good source of folate, which is needed for healthy DNA formation and reproductive function, and contains fiber, which helps to keep cholesterol levels low and prevent heart disease.

TANGY CITRUS JUICE

serves 1-2

2 oranges
1 grapefruit
1 lemon
1 lime

Peel and slice the fruits, and press alternate pieces of each through a juicer. Drink immediately.

Lime can help to speed up the body's natural healing process.

strawberry

These favorite summer berries were prized for their therapeutic properties in ancient Rome.

Packed with vitamin C, an average serving of strawberries gives twice the recommended daily adult intake of this immunity-boosting vitamin. The berries are also rich in fiber for a healthy heart and digestive system. Strawberries contain ellagic acid, a phytochemical shown to help fight cancer and destroy some of the toxins in cigarette smoke and polluted air. Their B-vitamin content makes them useful for supporting the nervous system and fighting stress-related conditions, as well as building resistance to disease.

NUTRIENTS Vitamins B3, B5, C; flavonoids; ellagic acid; fiber

Strawberries help to protect the skin's elasticity by supporting collagen production.

STRAWBERRY SMOOTHIE
serves 2

1 cup fresh strawberries, hulled
1 banana, peeled and chopped
1 cup plain bio-yoghurt
1 cup unsweetened soya milk
fresh mint leaves, to decorate

Place all the ingredients in a blender and whizz until smooth. Serve in tall glasses topped with mint leaves.

blueberry

NUTRIENTS Vitamins B2, C, E, beta-carotene, folate; anthocyanins, ellagic acid, tannins; fiber

Popular in the US, these juicy berries get full marks for their health-giving properties.

Native to North America, blueberries have been used medicinally for centuries by Native North Americans, while members of the same plant family are known throughout the world for their healing abilities. They taste similar to blackcurrants, but without the sharpness. Blueberries are often stewed and sweetened, but for their full range of health benefits they are best eaten raw.

BLUEBERRIES' IMMUNITY-BOOSTING PROPERTIES

One serving of blueberries provides as many antioxidants as five servings of broccoli, apples, or carrots, and studies have ranked them above all other fruit and vegetables for antioxidant activity. Ellagic acid, one of these antioxidants, is thought to prevent the development of cancer. Blueberries also contain the antioxidant anthocyanins, which strengthen blood capillaries, improving circulation and helping the transport of nutrients around the body – probably one of the reasons blueberries can enhance eyesight and protect against dementia, heart disease, and strokes. They have an anti-inflammatory effect on the body's tissues, and are rich in tannins, which fight the bacteria that cause urinary tract infections.

USING BLUEBERRIES

Eat blueberries three or four times a week for full immunity-boosting benefits. They can be eaten raw as a snack, with plain bio-yoghurt and nuts for a light breakfast, or combined with other berries and a little cream for a delicious dessert.

BLUEBERRY FACTS

• Native North Americans and early European settlers used blueberry root as a relaxant during childbirth. They also treated coughs with the juice, and made tea from the leaves to help to purify the blood.

• Eating blueberries stains the tongue blue, owing to its health-giving anthocyanin pigment, which is water soluble.

• When cooked or dried much of the vitamin-C content in blueberries is destroyed, although they retain their flavonoid activity.

BLUEBERRY SMOOTHIE *serves 2–3*

2 cups blueberries **1 cup raspberries or** **other summer berries** **1 cup plain bio-** **yoghurt**	Whizz together in a blender, then serve. When temperatures outside are sizzling, simply add 4 cubes of ice to the berries in the blender to make a cooling summer crush.

cherry

NUTRIENTS Vitamin C; potassium; anthocyanins, ellagic acid

These sweet summer treats are potent detoxifiers and are useful in the prevention of cancer.

Like many other berries, cherries contain ellagic acid – a powerful compound that blocks an enzyme that cancer cells need in order to develop. Cherries are also rich in anthocyanins, antioxidant substances that the body uses to help make disease-fighting chemicals, and they contain immune-essential vitamin C, and so can aid the fight against viruses and bacteria. In addition, they have anti-inflammatory properties, which ease rheumatoid arthritis and gout.

Infusions made from cherry stalks are a traditional remedy for cystitis.

CHOCO-CHERRIES
serves 2–4

½ lb cherries, left on
the stalk
4 squares good quality plain
chocolate, melted

Dip each of the cherries into the chocolate. Place on a greased plate and chill until set.

044

raspberry

These jewel-like, soft berries are effective fighters of infection, cancer and heart disease.

One of the top fruit sources of fiber, raspberries are helpful for keeping cholesterol low and improving digestion, as well as detoxifying the body. They contain high levels of infection-fighting vitamin C and manganese and, like other berries, are high in anthocyanins, powerful antioxidants that help the body to produce cells to fight off unwanted invaders. Raspberries have anti-cancer properties, and may be especially useful for preventing cancers of the mouth, throat, and colon.

NUTRIENTS Vitamins B3, C, biotin, folate; iron, manganese; anthocyanins; fiber

Raspberries perish quickly, so ideally buy them on the day on which you plan to eat them.

RASPBERRY BRULÉE
serves 4

3 cups fresh raspberries
1¼ cups plain bio-yoghurt
1 tsp vanilla extract
6 tsp raw cane sugar

Place the raspberries in 4 ramekins or small dishes. Combine the vanilla extract and yoghurt and spoon the mixture over the fruit. Cover the surface of each ramekin with the sugar, then caramelize under a very hot broiler for 2 minutes, or until crisp. Let cool, then serve.

cranberry

NUTRIENTS Vitamin C; iron; tannins

These tart, tangy berries are high in antioxidant vitamin C, making them great immunity-boosters.

Cranberries have natural anti-bacterial properties and are perhaps best known for helping to treat and prevent cystitis. It is thought that the condensed tannins they contain prevent bacteria from sticking to the walls of the urinary tract. Rich in vitamin C, cranberries can also ward off colds and 'flu. If you have difficulty finding the fresh berries, buy dried cranberries, juice or extract instead. For maximum benefit drink a glass of cranberry juice or take 800mg of extract daily.

CRANBERRY CRUSH
serves 2

1¾ cups fresh cranberries
juice of 2 oranges
juice of 1 grapefruit
2 bananas
ice, to serve

Whizz all the ingredients together in a blender, top with the ice and serve in tall glasses.

Whenever possible, drink unsweetened cranberry juice, as sugar suppresses the immune system.

rosehip

Packed with vitamin C, this little seed pod can be highly effective in staving off colds and 'flu.

Rosehips are actually the seed pods of roses and appear on rose bushes after they have flowered. They contain twenty times more vitamin C than oranges by weight, and therefore help to improve resistance to infections, such as the common cold, by enhancing the cleaning action of phagocytes (white blood cells) and detoxifying bacteria. Rosehips are also a good source of pectin, a type of fiber that binds to cholesterol and toxins to carry them out of the body.

During World War II, children in Britain were given rosehip syrup to prevent vitamin C deficiency.

NUTRIENTS Vitamin C, carotenoids; fiber

ROSEHIP SYRUP
makes 1 bottle

¼ lb rosehips
2¼ cups water
⅓ cup raw cane sugar

Place the rosehips and water in a saucepan, bring to a boil, then let cool. Strain through cheesecloth several times to remove seeds, sharp fibers, and pulp. Bring the strained liquid back to a boil, add the sugar, and simmer until the volume is reduced by about a third. Cool and pour into a small sterile bottle.

047

C ◎ ♡
hazelnut

NUTRIENTS Vitamins B1, B3, B6, E, folate; iron, calcium, magnesium, manganese, potassium; omega-9 fatty acids; protein

Dense in healthy oils as well as tasty, hazelnuts make a nutritious snack.

Hazelnuts are particularly high in healthy omega-9 fatty acids. They also contain good levels of antioxidant vitamin E, which helps to protect the body from the effects of pollution and other toxins, and vitamin B6, which is needed to make cysteine, a key amino acid for the immune system. Hazelnuts are also rich in important minerals, including iron and calcium, and they are a good source of essential protein.

Hazelnuts contain an amino acid that can activate cold sores, so avoid them if you are prone to these blisters.

HAZELNUT BUTTER *makes 1 small bowl*

2 cups hazelnuts, shelled
2 tbsp sunflower oil
1 tsp raw cane sugar, to taste

Put the shelled nuts on a baking sheet and place in a hot oven to cook for 20 minutes or until the skins crack. Remove from the oven. Rub the skins off with a rough cloth, then place them in a blender with 1 tbsp of the oil. Whizz until a chunky paste forms, then add the remaining oil and the sugar. Blend again until smooth.

walnut

These subtly flavored nuts are full of nutrients.

Walnuts contain glutathione, an important antioxidant that aids the development of lymphocyte immune cells. They are rich in alpha-linoleic acid (an omega-6 fatty acid) which helps reduce cholesterol levels and boost heart health, and their B-vitamins can provide energy and improve brain function. Their high vitamin E content also makes them a good choice for maintaining healthy skin.

Eating just ¼ cup of walnuts a day provides half your daily quota of essential alpha-linoleic acid.

NUTRIENTS Vitamins B1, B2, B3, B5, B6, E, folate; calcium, iron, selenium, zinc; glutathione; omega-6 and -9 fatty acids

WALNUT PASTA SALAD
serves 4

4 tbsp walnuts, chopped
12oz wholewheat pasta spirals, cooked
3 large tomatoes, cut into wedges
a handful of arugula
2 tbsp fresh basil
1 clove garlic, crushed
4 tbsp walnut oil
2 tbsp balsamic vinegar

In a large bowl, combine all the ingredients except the garlic, oil and vinegar. Whisk these remaining ingredients together, then drizzle over the salad. Serve immediately.

⊙ ⊙ ♥

cashew nut

NUTRIENTS Vitamins B2, B3, B5, B6, biotin, folate; iodine, iron, magnesium, manganese, potassium, selenium, zinc; protein

These seeds of the Brazilian "cashew apple" are full of healthy fats that can lower cholesterol.

Cashew nuts are a rich source of B-vitamins, which aid the maintainance of the body's nerves and muscle tissue, and boost resistance to stress. They also contain minerals important for immune health, including the antioxidant selenium, which is crucial in the production of antibodies, and virus-fighting zinc, which helps to keep cancer cells at bay. In addition, cashews contain mono-unsaturated fats – these have been shown to help keep cholesterol levels down.

Cashew nuts are a good source of protein, making an ideal snack to stave off hunger pangs.

SUMMER BERRIES WITH CASHEW CREAM *serves 4*

1 cup cashew nuts, shelled
½ cup water
1 tsp ground nutmeg
2 tbsp runny honey
2 cups raspberries
2 cups strawberries, hulled and halved

Blend the nuts and water in a food processor until smooth, then add the nutmeg and honey and whizz again until thoroughly blended. Divide the berries into 4 bowls, top with the cashew cream, and serve.

050

pine nut

Full of protein and minerals, these aromatic kernels can aid the prevention of disease.

As well as being rich in the immunity-boosting antioxidant mineral zinc, pine nuts contain high levels of anti-inflammatory polyunsaturated fats, which help to maintain low cholesterol and promote a healthy heart. They are high in vitamin E, which helps protect against the damage that can be caused by pollution and other toxins, and is needed by the immune system's antibodies to fight disease. Pine nuts are also a good source of magnesium, which helps to calm allergic reactions.

Pine nuts can be sprinkled into salads and stir-fries to add a protein kick.

NUTRIENTS Vitamins B1, B2, B3; E; iron, magnesium, manganese, zinc; protein

RED PEPPER BRUSCHETTA
serves 4

4 red bell peppers, cored and sliced
1 clove garlic, crushed
1 tbsp balsamic vinegar
5 tbsp olive oil
1 wholewheat loaf, sliced thickly
½ lb goats' cheese
½ cup pine nuts, toasted

Broil the bell peppers until soft, then place in a bowl and toss with the garlic, vinegar and 4 tbsp of the oil. Drizzle the remaining oil over the bread, and place in a hot oven to bake until golden on each side, turning once. Top each slice with goats' cheese, bell peppers and pine nuts.

Brazil nut

NUTRIENTS Vitamins B1, E, biotin; calcium, iron, magnesium, selenium, zinc; omega-6 fatty acids; glutathione, fiber, protein

High in the antioxidant mineral selenium, the Brazil is one of the most nutritious of all nuts.

The Brazil nut grows wild in the Amazonian rainforest, where it was sacred to ancient tribes. It is the kernel of a fruit that loosely resembles a coconut, and the nuts grow in clusters of up to 24 within this shell. When ripe, the shells fall to the ground. The kernels are then removed, dried in the sun, and washed before being exported.

BRAZIL NUT'S IMMUNITY-BOOSTING PROPERTIES

This nut is one of the best sources of selenium, an antioxidant mineral that strengthens the immune system's antibody response and helps to prevent cancer, heart disease and, premature ageing. It is a key component in the action of glutathione, an enzyme that suppresses free radicals and helps to halt the development of tumors. Brazil nuts are packed with vitamin E, which works with selenium to provide a super-boost to the immune system. They also contain other important minerals, including magnesium and iron, and are rich in omega-6 fatty acids – essential for easing inflammation in the body, enhancing digestion, and improving the skin.

USING BRAZIL NUTS

Rich in protein, a handful of Brazil nuts eaten raw makes a satisfying snack. They can be processed into nut milk or butter, and can be used in stir-fries and salads to add a crunchy protein kick.

BRAZIL NUT FACTS

• Brazil nuts are a vital source of income to the population of the Amazonian rainforest, from where they are most commonly exported to Europe and North America.

• The Brazil nut is also known as the para nut, cream nut (because of its rich flavour) and castanaea.

• After Brazil nuts have been collected, the fibrous, woody capsules that contain the kernels are used as animal traps.

• Brazil nuts have a high fat content, so will turn rancid very quickly and should not be stored for long periods. As with all nuts and seeds are best stored in the fridge.

GREEN BEAN AND BRAZIL NUT STIR-FRY *serves 4*

2 tbsp sesame oil
1 onion, chopped
1 tbsp grated fresh ginger
2 cloves garlic, crushed
½ lb asparagus spears
½ lb green beans
¼ cup Brazil nuts, sliced
2 tbsp soy sauce

Heat the sesame oil in a wok over a high heat until it is sizzling hot, then add the onion, ginger, and garlic. Stir-fry for 2 minutes, then add the asparagus spears, green beans, and Brazil nuts. Continue to stir-fry for a further 5 minutes, then add the soy sauce. Reduce

the heat and cook slowly until the asparagus and beans are tender – this should take 8–10 minutes. Serve immediately on a bed of brown rice.

○ ◉ ⏷ ♡

pistachio nut

NUTRIENTS Vitamins B1, B3, E; magnesium, manganese, potassium, calcium; omega-9 fatty acids; protein

These distinctive pale-green nuts are a popular snack and high in beneficial minerals.

Pistachio nuts contain the anti-viral mineral calcium, which we need to activate the action of phagocytic cells. They are rich in magnesium, which helps the body to absorb calcium, and eases allergic reactions. Pistachios also contain high levels of nutritious monounsaturated fats plus vitamin E, which helps to detoxify the body, and are a good source of B-vitamins, essential for healthy nerve and muscle tissue.

PISTACHIO SALAD *serves 4*

1 clove garlic, crushed
1 tsp Dijon mustard
1 tbsp balsamic vinegar
juice of 1 orange
¼ lb watercress
¼ lb arugula
1 green apple, cored and diced
8 tbsp pistachio nuts, shelled

In a bowl, whisk together the garlic, mustard, balsamic vinegar and, orange juice to make the dressing. Set to one side. Place the watercress and arugula on serving plates and sprinkle over the apple and pistachios evenly. Drizzle with the dressing, and serve.

Ⓒ ⊙ ♡

almond

These strongly-flavored nuts contain healthy oils and other vitality-enhancing nutrients.

Almonds are one of the top sources of cancer-preventing antioxidant vitamin E, containing 24mg per 100g as well as being a good source of the anti-viral mineral calcium. They also provide laetrile, thought to be a powerful tumor-fighting compound, and are rich in zinc, which helps to build up immune strength and improve wound healing. Rich in nutritious monounsaturated fats, almonds can also help to lower cholesterol levels.

NUTRIENTS Vitamins B2, B5, E, biotin; calcium, iron, magnesium, phosphorous, potassium, zinc; laetrile; omega-9 fatty acids

> Almonds are an excellent skin food, providing vitamin E and zinc, which are both crucial for a healthy complexion.

ALMOND BANANA SMOOTHIE *serves 2*

1 cup blanched almonds
2 small bananas
2¼ cups water
a pinch of cinnamon
2 tsp vanilla extract
2 tsp honey

Place the almonds, bananas, and water in a blender and whizz until smooth. Add the vanilla extract, honey, and cinnamon and whizz again. Serve.

054

sunflower seed and oil

NUTRIENTS Vitamins E, B1, B2, B3; calcium, copper, magnesium, manganese, iron, selenium, zinc; omega-6 fatty acids; protein

This tasty seed and its oil are bursting with health-giving properties.

Sunflower seeds contain minerals important for immunity, including magnesium, which helps to calm allergic reactions and zinc, a powerful anti-viral mineral. They are also rich in vitamin E, an antioxidant which prevents the damage caused by harmful toxins, and keeps skin and cell tissue healthy. Their B-vitamin content makes sunflower seeds effective in aiding the body to cope with stress. As sunflower oil is a polyunsaturate it should never be heated and only cold-pressed varieties used.

MUESLI *serves 4*

1½ cups rolled oats
2 tbsp dried dates, chopped
2 tbsp dried apricots, chopped
1 tbsp pecan nuts, chopped
1 tbsp almonds, flaked
1 tbsp sunflower seeds
1 tbsp linseeds
1 tbsp wheatgerm
1 tbsp wheat bran
2 apples, peeled, cored and chopped
unsweetened soy milk, to serve

Combine all the dry ingredients in a bowl and top with the apple. Serve with the soy milk.

Sunflower oil is a useful kitchen basic and ideal for use in salad dressings.

© ✋ ⓞ ♡

pumpkin seed

These seeds are richer in iron than any other.

Pumpkin seeds are a good source of both omega-3 and omega-6 fatty acids. They are crucial for good immune function, as well as for healthy skin, blood clotting, digestion, and nerve function. They are also rich in B-vitamins, important for moderating stress and its damaging effects on immunity, and contain many other minerals that support the immune system, including the antioxidant minerals selenium, and zinc.

NUTRIENTS Vitamins B1, B2, B3; iron, magnesium, phosphorous, potassium, selenium, zinc; omega-3 and -6 fatty acids; protein

Pumpkin seeds are a good source of protein and can help to regulate blood sugar levels.

GREEK PEAR DESSERT *serves 2*

2 ripe pears, chopped
1 cup Greek yoghurt
3 tbsp pumpkin seeds
1 tbsp sunflower seeds
1 tbsp manuka or
    runny honey

Divide the chopped pear between 2 bowls and top with the yoghurt. Sprinkle the seeds in a layer over the yoghurt, then drizzle over the honey, and serve.

safflower oil

NUTRIENTS Vitamin E; phytosterols; omega-6 fatty acids

This light, golden oil comes from the seeds of the safflower.

Safflower oil is dense in vitamin E, an antioxidant which helps to ward off cancer, keep skin healthy, and detoxify the body. It also contains phytosterols, plant chemicals that can help to lower cholesterol and therefore help prevent heart disease and strokes. Safflower oil is rich in omega-6 fatty acids, which the body converts into prostaglandins that balance the immune system and stop allergic reactions, as well as thin the blood, soothe inflammation, improve nerve and brain function and aid the regulation of blood sugar levels. It is a polyunsaturate so it should not be heated and cold-pressed varieties always used.

SAFFLOWER VINAIGRETTE *makes 1 small bowl*

¼ cup white wine vinegar
2 tsp Dijon mustard
kosher salt and black
 pepper, to taste
⅔ cup safflower oil

Whisk the vinegar, mustard, salt, and pepper together in a bowl. Slowly drizzle in the oil, whisking until the ingredients are thoroughly combined. Use immediately, or store in a jar. Shake well before use.

○ ● ◍ ◎

evening primrose oil

This healing flower oil stabilizes hormones and boosts skin health.

NUTRIENTS Vitamin E; gamma linoleic acid; omega-6 fatty acids

Evening primrose oil is one of the richest known direct sources of gamma linoleic acid (GLA), an omega-6 fatty acid. In the body, this substance is converted into prostaglandins, hormone-like substances which help to regulate the immune system, thin the blood, decrease inflammation and improve nerve and muscle function. Increasing the body's levels of prostaglandins may also ease PMS symptoms. In addition, evening primrose oil is rich in vitamin E, which can help to boost skin health and ease conditions such as eczema.

EVENING PRIMROSE SALAD DRESSING *makes 1 small bowl*

1 tbsp balsamic vinegar
3 tbsp lemon juice
1 tsp wholegrain mustard
1 tbsp fresh parsley, chopped
1 tbsp fresh chives, chopped
1 clove garlic, chopped
1 tsp dried oregano
1 tsp dried basil
3 tbsp evening primrose oil

a pinch of cayenne pepper
kosher salt, to taste

In a blender, combine the vinegar, mustard, herbs and garlic. Blend until smooth. Slowly add the oil, then blend again until creamy. Season with cayenne and salt.

Ⓒ Ⓞ ◐

sesame seed and oil

NUTRIENTS Vitamins B1, B2, B3, E; calcium, iron, zinc; omega-6 and -9 fatty acids

These tiny seeds can add both taste and essential nutrients to a variety of sweet and savory dishes.

Add sesame seeds to salads and smoothies for a protein boost.

Sesame seeds have a nutty flavor and are slightly crunchy in texture to eat. Valuable health-boosters, they are made into a number of products such as sesame oil, which is highly resistant to rancidity, and tahini, a sesame-seed paste. Rich in immunity-fortifying zinc and antioxidant vitamin E, they also contain B-vitamins to support the nervous system and to help the body cope with stress. A good source of vegetarian protein, sesame seeds are packed with omega-6 fatty acids for healthy skin and circulation.

CRUNCHY SESAME STIR-FRY *serves 4*

3 tbsp olive oil
2 tbsp sesame seeds
1 x 2-inch piece fresh ginger, peeled and grated
2 cloves garlic, crushed
½ a head of broccoli, broken into small florets
3 carrots, cut into long thin slices
½ cabbage, shredded

In a wok, heat the oil and sesame seeds until the seeds start to toast. Then add the ginger and garlic, followed by the other ingredients. Combine well. Turn the heat down to low and fry for a further 5–10 minutes. Serve.

aduki bean

These nutty beans, known as the "king of beans" in Japan, are packed with energizing nutrients.

Aduki beans are high in fiber, making them useful for speeding up the elimination of waste and helping to detoxify the body. They contain good levels of B-vitamins, which are needed for steady energy production and to repair body tissues. Aduki beans are also a useful source of protein, which helps to build muscle and maintain healthy skin, and are rich in immunity minerals including anti-viral zinc, calcium, and magnesium.

NUTRIENTS Vitamins B1, B2, B3; calcium, magnesium, manganese, zinc; fiber, protein

ADUKI BEAN CASSEROLE
serves 2

1 red onion, chopped
2 tbsp olive oil
1 red bell pepper, chopped
1 stick celery, chopped
2 carrots, chopped
2 large tomatoes, chopped
1 heaped cup aduki beans, soaked overnight
1 clove garlic, crushed
1 tsp ground cumin
1 tsp fennel seeds
1 tsp ground coriander
2½ cups vegetable stock

In a wok, gently fry the onion in the olive oil until soft and golden. Add the bell pepper, celery, carrots, and tomatoes, and stir-fry for 2 minutes. Add the beans, garlic, and spices. Stir, pour on the stock and simmer for 30 minutes. Serve with brown rice.

Aduki beans are also known as adzuki or azuki beans.

oats

NUTRIENTS Vitamins B1, B2, B3, B5, E, folate; iron, magnesium, selenium, silica, zinc; flavonoids; fiber, protein

Comforting and sustaining, oats also bring a host of health benefits.

Oats are high in immunity-boosting vitamin E and contain flavonoids called avenanthramides – potent antioxidants which help to break down cholesterol build-up and are thought to help prevent cancer, especially colon cancer. Oats are high in fiber, so have laxative properties, and are also rich in silica, an anti-inflammatory mineral which soothes the digestive tract. Packed with B vitamins, oats are useful for easing stress, and can aid weight loss as they release their energy slowly, staving off hunger pangs.

Oats can be used to ease eczema – tie a muslin bag of oats over the tap when running a bath and soak in the water.

FRUITY SOY PORRIDGE *serves 2*

3¾ cups unsweetened
 soy milk
1½ cups oats
1 tsp ground cinnamon
1 small banana, chopped
1¾ cups blueberries
2 tbsp flaked almonds

Put the soy milk and oats in a saucepan and cook over a low heat, stirring regularly, for 5 minutes. Add the cinnamon and banana, stir, and cook for 2 minutes. Divide mixture into 2 bowls. Serve topped with the blueberries and flaked almonds.

wheat germ

This tiny wheat seed is surprisingly rich in essential nutrients.

Found inside the wheat grain, wheat germ is rich in the antioxidant vitamin E, which helps to detoxify the body by neutralizing harmful free radicals. It is also an excellent source of a range of B-vitamins, which are needed by the body's cells to fight disease as well as to maintain healthy nerves and mucous membranes. Wheat germ is a very high-fiber food, and so helps to ensure an efficient digestive system as well as reduce cholesterol levels.

NUTRIENTS Vitamins B1, B2, B3, B5, B6, E, folate; iron, magnesium, manganese, selenium, zinc; fiber

You should avoid wheat germ if you are allergic to wheat or gluten.

HONEY WHEAT GERM SMOOTHIE *serves 1*

1 cup soy milk
¼ cup plain bio-yoghurt
1 cup strawberries, hulled
1 large ripe banana
2 tsp wheat germ
2 tsp manuka honey

Whizz all the ingredients together in a blender, and serve immediately.

062

bulgur

NUTRIENTS Vitamins B1, B2, B3; copper, iron, magnesium, phosphorous; protein, fiber

A mineral-rich grain made from wheat berries, bulgur makes a good alternative to rice.

A cracked wheat grain, bulgur is dense in digestion-boosting fiber, which is also needed to keep blood cholesterol low. It is a good source of B-vitamins, which help the body to mop up invader cells, as well as stabilizing energy levels and maintaining a healthy nervous system. Bulgur also contains minerals including iron, important for increasing overall resistance to infection.

BULGUR-STUFFED VINE LEAVES *serves 4*

½ cup boiling water
1 cup bulgur
1 small onion, sliced
3 tsp olive oil
1 tsp cumin seeds
½ cup firm tofu, grated
6 sun-dried tomatoes, chopped
1 tsp fresh mint, chopped
½ tsp lemon juice
black pepper, to taste
16 vine leaves, blanched for
   5 minutes

Pour the water onto the bulgur and set aside for 20 minutes. In a saucepan, fry the onion in the oil until golden, then stir in the cumin seeds. Remove from the heat and add the bulgur, tofu, tomatoes, mint, lemon juice and pepper. Divide the mixture among the vine leaves, roll and secure with a cocktail stick. Steam for 20 minutes, and serve.

Bulgur is unsuitable for people who suffer from a wheat or gluten allergy.

quinoa

Known as the "mother grain" by the Incas, these bead-shaped grains are packed with goodness.

Often called a "perfect food", quinoa is a complete protein which means that it contains all 8 essential amino acids, an extremely rare quality in the plant world. Quinoa is also a good source of antioxidant vitamin E, needed for the body's healing processes, and contains a number of immunity-enhancing minerals, including zinc, which is necessary for the health of the thymus gland – the regulator of immune cell production.

Quinoa's fiber content makes it helpful for boosting digestion and relieving constipation.

NUTRIENTS Vitamins B2, B3, E; iron, calcium, magnesium zinc; saponins; fiber, protein

QUINOA PILAFF
serves 4

3¾ cups water
¾ lb quinoa
⅔ cup olive oil
1lb okra, sliced finely
3 tbsp tomato paste
1 onion, chopped
2 cloves garlic, crushed
2 tsp cumin seeds
1 tsp black pepper
½ cup cilantro, chopped

Boil the water in a saucepan. Add the quinoa, bring to the boil again and simmer for 15 minutes. Drain. Heat the oil in a wok, add the okra and stir-fry for 3 minutes. Add the other ingredients apart from the cilantro and quinoa, and stir-fry for 5 minutes. Lower the heat and cook for a further 10 minutes. Mix in the quinoa and cilantro. Serve.

◯ ⓒ ◉ ⊜ ♡

rice

NUTRIENTS Vitamins B1, B3, folate; iron, magnesium, manganese, phosphorous, copper, zinc; complex carbohydrates, fiber, protein

The second most widely cultivated grain in the world is a powerhouse of nutrients.

Always choose brown rice, which is richer in nutrients than the processed, white variety.

Brown rice is dense in B-vitamins, which are needed for a healthy brain and nervous system, while its protein levels help to build muscles, skin, and hair. It is also a good source of zinc and trace minerals, such as magnesium, phosphorus and copper, which all build resistance to infections. Rice's rich fiber content is excellent for the digestive system and helps to lower cholesterol, so is important for a healthy heart. It is a complex carbohydrate, so it releases energy slowly, and is ideal for keeping hunger pangs at bay.

BROWN RICE SALAD *serves 1–2*

⅓ cup brown rice, cooked
   and cooled
2 scallions, sliced
4 tomatoes, cut into segments
½ cup black olives,
   pitted and halved
2 cloves garlic, crushed
3 tbsp fresh basil, roughly

chopped
3 tbsp olive oil

Combine all the ingredients in a large salad bowl. Leave, un-refrigerated, for 1 hour to allow the flavours to mingle, then serve.

◐ ◉ ◉ ♡

corn

Also known as maize, this staple food is particularly rich in immunity-bolstering vitamins.

NUTRIENTS Vitamins A, B3, B5, C, beta-carotene, folate; magnesium, zinc; fiber

Canned and frozen sweetcorn retains most of the nutrients found in the fresh cobs.

Corn can be ground into meal and used as a flour, but the most nutritious form is as the kernels that grow on sweetcorn ears. These contain good levels of vitamin C, which helps to strengthen the immune system to fight viruses and bacteria, and is an excellent source of fiber, which is important for lowering blood cholesterol and helping to prevent heart disease. Folate, needed for reproductive health, is found in corn, along with other B-vitamins that are useful for boosting energy and resistance to stress.

CORN FRITTERS serves 2

1 cup wholewheatl flour
2 eggs
1¼ cups milk
2 tbsp fresh cilantro, chopped
2 cups corn kernels, fresh
   or canned
black pepper, to taste
2 tbsp olive oil

Whisk the flour, eggs and, milk into a smooth batter, then add the cilantro, sweetcorn and, pepper. Heat the olive oil in a skillet, divide the mixture into 8 small patties, and fry until golden on both sides. Serve.

black-eyed bean

NUTRIENTS Vitamins B1, B2, B3, biotin, folate; calcium, iron, magnesium, manganese, selenium, zinc; fiber, protein

This highly nutritious bean is an essential ingredient in Creole and Cajun cooking.

Black-eyed beans contain zinc, an important antioxidant mineral that helps the development of the body's disease-fighting cells. They also contain selenium, another antioxidant mineral which is needed to produce antibodies and to help to prevent cancer. The beans are rich in energy-boosting B-vitamins, including folate, which is necessary for healthy reproductive organs. They are also a good source of protein, used for building muscle and increasing vitality, and fibre, for a healthy digestive system and heart.

BLACK-EYED BEAN RICE *serves 4*

5 scallions, chopped
2 tsp olive oil
2 cups black-eyed beans, cooked
2 tbsp water
juice of 1 lime
½ tsp chili powder
½ tsp cumin
2 tbsp cilantro, chopped
¾ cup basmati rice, cooked

black pepper, to taste

In a skillet gently fry the onions in the oil until golden. Add all the remaining ingredients, apart from the rice, stir and heat through for 2 minutes. Add the rice and black pepper and stir-fry for a further 2 minutes, then serve immediately.

kidney bean

Widely used in South America, these soft beans are high in protein, vitamins, and minerals.

Kidney beans are rich in folate, a B-vitamin that is important for good reproductive health and efficient wound healing. They are an excellent source of protein, which helps to keep energy levels steady, and contain high levels of fiber, which is vital for keeping blood cholesterol low, and good digestion. Kidney beans also contain iron – essential for the production of the immune system's antibodies and white blood cells.

Kidney beans are highly toxic if eaten raw, so always choose cooked or canned beans.

NUTRIENTS Folate; potassium, iron, manganese; fiber, protein

QUICK KIDNEY BEAN CASSEROLE serves 2

2 tbsp olive oil
2¼ cups kidney beans, canned
3 large ripe tomatoes,chopped
1 red bell pepper, chopped
1 onion, chopped
2 cloves garlic, crushed
1 zucchini, sliced
4 portabello mushrooms, sliced
2 tsp fresh basil, chopped
1 tsp kosher salt

Heat the olive oil in a large saucepan, then add the onion and fry until golden. Add the pepper, zucchini, mushrooms, tomato and garlic, stir for 5 minutes, then add the kidney beans, and enough water to cover. Add the basil and salt, then cover and simmer until the vegetables are soft. Serve with brown rice.

lima bean

This soft, floury bean is rich in B-vitamins and is a good source of protein.

NUTRIENTS Vitamins B3, B5, folate; iron, manganese, potassium, zinc; fiber, protein

Dried lima beans have high levels of vitamin B5, an important immune stimulant that helps the body to produce antibodies to fight off disease. They are also a useful source of folate, another B-vitamin that is vital for good reproductive health. In addition, lima beans are rich in minerals, and have some manganese, which works to help stop viruses developing, as well as immune-fortifying iron and zinc.

MIDDLE-EASTERN STYLE LIMA BEANS *serves 4*

1 onion, chopped
1 tsp ground cinnamon
2 tbsp olive oil
1lb lima beans,
    cooked or canned
1 tsp salt
sprinkling black pepper
½ tsp mild chili powder
1¾ cups water
½ lb canned tomatoes,
    chopped
4 cloves garlic, crushed
juice of ½ a lemon
a handful of fresh parsley,
    roughly chopped

Sauté the onion and cinnamon in the oil, then add the beans, salt, pepper, chili powder and water. Bring to the boil, reduce the heat and simmer for 15 minutes. Add the tomatoes, garlic and, lemon juice and simmer for another 5 minutes. Serve garnished with parsley.

Dried lima beans are helpful for maintaining healthy skin and hair.

lentil

The humble lentil, one of our oldest foods and a staple in many countries, is antioxidant-rich.

Lentils are rich in B-vitamins, which help to boost the body's immune system, aiding the fighting of bacteria and other invaders. They contain minerals important for immunity too, including antioxidant selenium and iron, which is vital for healthy blood. Along with all other pulses, lentils contain anti-carcinogenic phytochemicals and are also a good source of plant oestrogens. Lentils can help to boost energy and as they are rich in fiber, they can improve heart and digestive health.

Green or brown lentils have higher levels of nutrients than the red variety.

NUTRIENTS Vitamins B3, B5, B6, folate; calcium, iron, magnesium, manganese, potassium, selenium, zinc; fiber, protein

WARM LENTIL SALAD
serves 4

- 1½ cups green or red lentils
- ¼ cup olive oil
- 2 onions, chopped
- 1 clove garlic, crushed
- 1 red bell pepper, chopped finely
- 1 zucchini, chopped finely
- 1 carrot, sliced finely
- 1 celery stick, chopped finely
- 2 large ripe tomatoes, deseeded and chopped
- 2 tbsp balsamic vinegar
- 1 tbsp fresh mint, finely chopped

Cook the lentils in boiling water for 10 minutes, or until just tender, then drain. Heat the oil in a wok and add all of the vegetables, stir-fry until tender. Remove from the heat, add the lentils, vinegar and, mint, combine thoroughly, and serve.

garbanzo

NUTRIENTS Vitamins B2, B3, B5, E, folate; iron, potassium, zinc; fiber, protein

Robust and hearty, garbanzos have a nutty flavour and a surprisingly creamy texture.

Garbanzos contain protease inhibitors, which halt the DNA-destroying action of cancer cells. They are rich in antioxidant vitamin E, which promotes the ability of white blood cells to fight infection, and zinc, needed for healthy cell growth. Garbanzos are also a good source of isoflavones, plant chemicals that are converted in the gut into a substance that mimics the hormone oestrogen, helping to prevent oestrogen-related conditions such as PMS and breast cancer. High in fibre and flavonoids, garbanzos help to keep the digestive system healthy and to lower cholesterol.

BELL PEPPER HOUMOUS
makes 1 bowl

2 cups garbanzos (either canned, pre-soaked, or sprouted for three days)
2 cloves garlic, crushed
3 tbsp tahini
juice of 3 large lemons
2 tsp tamari soy sauce
1 red bell pepper, chopped

Place all the ingredients in a blender and combine thoroughly into a smooth paste. Add a little water if the mixture is too thick. Use as a dip with oatcakes or chopped raw vegetables, or as a side dressing with salad. Houmous will keep for up to 3 days in the fridge.

Sprouted garbanzos contain more nutrients than the soaked or canned varieties.

green bean

Crunchy green beans are rich in disease-fighting vitamins and minerals.

Like other pulses, green beans are low in fat and high in soluble fiber, which is important for a healthy heart. They have high levels of B-vitamins, needed for the development of phagocyte cells, which mop up unwanted invaders, and also contain beta-carotene, which the body converts to cancer-preventing vitamin A. Green beans are also a good source of manganese, needed for the production of the anti-viral substance interferon.

NUTRIENTS Vitamins B3, folate, beta-carotene; iron, manganese; fiber

Choose fresh, firm green beans as these contain the highest levels of nutrients.

BEAN AND RICE SALAD
serves 4

- 1¼ cups Arborio rice, cooked and cooled
- 1¼ cups green beans, chopped
- 1 bunch of asparagus, cut into small pieces
- 1 cup canned kidney beans, drained
- 1 red bell pepper, finely chopped
- 20 green olives, pitted
- 3 tbsp fresh parsley, chopped
- 3 tbsp fresh mint, chopped
- 5 scallions, chopped
- 3 tbsp white wine vinegar
- 2 tbsp olive oil

Steam the green beans and asparagus until *al dente*. Let cool, and place in a bowl with the rice. Mix well, then add the remaining ingredients. Combine thoroughly and let stand for 1 hour, then serve.

© ◑ ◎ ⇎ ♡

*soy bean

This versatile food has medicinal qualities that can help to prevent diseases, especially cancer.

Soy bean is probably the most nutritious of all the pulses, and can be eaten in many different forms – as sprouts, tofu, tempeh, yoghurt, flour, milk, miso and soy sauce. It is a traditional food in Japan, where it is thought to have originated. The low levels of certain cancers among the Japanese have led to the properties of soy being studied in clinical research.

SOY BEAN'S IMMUNITY-BOOSTING PROPERTIES

Soy beans contain phytoestrogens called isoflavones, which can mimic the effects of the hormone oestrogen in the body. This makes them useful for helping to control menopausal symptoms, such as hot flushes, and studies have shown that isoflavones can help to prevent the hormone-linked diseases of breast and prostate cancer. The protease inhibitors found in soy beans also help to protect against cancer. In addition antioxidant vitamin E, which defends cells against free radical damage, is found in soy beans. They also contain B vitamins which play a role in maintaining the nervous system and helping the body to cope with stress.

USING SOY BEANS

Raw beans can take time to prepare, but using tofu and soy milk is easier and ensures that most of the nutrients are intact. Tofu can be used instead of meat or fish, while soy milk and yoghurt make healthy alternatives to their dairy counterparts.

SOY BEAN FACTS

• Soy is often genetically modified, so choose organic or guaranteed GM-free products.

• Soy beans contain more protein than dairy products, but none of the cholesterol.

• People who are allergic to soy might cross-react to foods such as peanuts, garbanzos, lima beans, wheat, rye and barley.

• Soy is one of the few foods of plant origin that contain all 8 essential amino acids.

• Fresh young soy beans are popular in Japan where they are boiled and served whole as an hors d'oeuvre or snack.

SCRAMBLED TOFU *serves 4*

1 tbsp soy sauce
1 tbsp fresh basil, finely
  chopped
1 tbsp fresh parsley, finely
  chopped
2 tbsp olive oil
2 scallions, sliced
½ lb soft tofu, crumbled

In a bowl, combine the soy sauce and herbs. Heat the olive oil in a skillet and fry the scallions until soft and golden. Stir in the tofu, then the soy sauce and herbs mixture, and stir-fry for 3 minutes. Serve on rye toast.

○ ○ ♡

snow pea

NUTRIENTS Vitamins B1, B2, B3, B5, C, beta-carotene, biotin; calcium, iron; fiber

These young pea pods have a delicate, sweet flavor as well as health benefits.

High in B-vitamins, snow peas help to maintain energy and build nerve and muscle tissue. They contain immunity-stimulant vitamin B5, and antioxidant vitamin C. Snow peas are also a good source of fiber, which helps lower cholesterol levels and promote an efficient digestive system.

SNOW PEA STIR-FRY
serves 4

2 tbsp sesame oil
1¼ lb firm tofu, cubed
2 tbsp butter
2 cloves garlic, crushed
2 red chilies, deseeded and
  finely chopped
2 tsp grated fresh ginger,
1½ lb snow peas
2 tbsp soy sauce

In a wok, heat half the sesame oil, then stir-fry the tofu until browned. Set aside. Add the remaining oil and butter to the wok, then stir-fry the garlic, chili and ginger. Add the snow peas, stir-frying until tender. Return the tofu to the wok, combine thoroughly, add the soy sauce and serve.

Snow peas are eaten whole and valued for their pods, rather than their peas.

turkey

Often reserved for festive occasions, nutritious turkey can be an everyday health-booster.

An excellent low-fat source of protein, turkey is rich in immunity-fortifying zinc, in a form that is easy for the body to use. It also contains selenium, which helps to repair cell DNA and lower the risk of cancer. Turkey is dense in B-vitamins, which are needed for a healthy nervous system and are important for keeping down levels of homocysteine in the blood. This is a toxic substance formed as a breakdown product of amino acids and linked with heart disease.

NUTRIENTS Vitamins B3, B6, B12; iron, selenium, zinc; protein

Dark turkey leg meat contains two times as much iron and three times as much zinc as white breast meat.

DELUXE TURKEY SANDWICH *serves 1*

½ avocado
2 slices wholewheat bread
fresh spinach leaves
cooked turkey slices
1 scallion, finely chopped
1 tomato, sliced
a little wholegrain mustard
  (optional)

Scoop out the avocado flesh and spread over the bread like butter. Layer the spinach and turkey slices on one slice and top with the scallion, tomato, and mustard, if desired. Sandwich together and eat immediately.

guinea fowl

This protein-rich meat is high in nutrients.

NUTRIENTS Vitamins B3, B6, B12; iron; protein

A small game bird thought to have originated in West Africa, guinea fowl is a healthy, low-fat source of protein. It contains good levels of vitamin B6, which is needed for the synthesis of cysteine, an important amino acid, and also to help eliminate waste matter from the body. As with all meat, guinea fowl contains vitamin B12, which helps maintain an efficient nervous system, and iron, which we need for healthy blood.

Choose organic guinea fowl, as conventional birds are farmed intensively and can be low in nutrients.

HERBY GUINEA FOWL *serves 2*

1 tbsp fresh parsley, chopped
1 tbsp fresh tarragon, chopped
2 guinea fowl breast halves
kosher salt and black pepper,
   to taste
2 tsp olive oil

Preheat the oven to 200°C/ 400°F/gas mark 6. Stuff the chopped herbs under the skin of the guinea fowl portions, and season as required. In a pan, heat the olive oil, and fry the breasts for 2 minutes on each side to brown, then transfer to the oven and cook for a further 8 minutes.

pheasant

Rich in B vitamins and protein, pheasant is a good source of energy.

NUTRIENTS Vitamins B2, B3, B6, B12; iron, potassium, zinc; protein

Pheasant is by far the most plentiful and popular of game birds. It is higher in fat than many other meats but the main fat it contains is the health-enhancing monounsaturated type, which is a plus. It also contains good levels of nutrients, so it is very beneficial when eaten occasionally. It is a useful source of vitamin B6, which is needed for the production of phagocytes to keep the body's cells healthy, and vitamins B2, B3 and B12 – vital for maintaining a healthy nervous system and consistent energy levels. It is also an excellent source of the immunity-boosting minerals, iron and zinc. However, pheasant is high in purines so should be avoided by those prone to gout.

Pheasant was originally introduced to Europe from China.

PHEASANT STIR-FRY
serves 2

2 pheasant breast halves, skinned
2 tbsp sesame oil
10 portobello mushrooms, sliced
1 red bell pepper, chopped
1 onion, chopped finely
2 tsp tamari soy sauce

Cut the pheasant portions into large pieces, then fry on a low heat in the oil until browned. Add the onion, bell pepper, and mushrooms and stir-fry together for around 6 minutes until the vegetables are tender and the pheasant cooked through. Add the soy sauce and serve with brown rice or noodles.

© ◎

duck

NUTRIENTS Vitamin B2; iron, zinc; protein

Duck is delicious roasted or stir-fried and is an excellent source of the stress-busting vitamin B2.

Duck is a popular and uniquely tasty variety of poultry and is a wonderful source of immune-boosting nutrients. Although duck is high in cholesterol, it is low in saturated fat. A skinless duck breast is leaner than a skinless chicken breast. Duck meat provides plenty of the protein and iron needed to repair tissue and build new cells. Eating duck will also help you to combat stress as it contains the vitamin B2 and aids the production of infection-fighting immune cells.

Ducks were first domesticated in China, where they are appreciated for their eggs.

GLAZED DUCK WITH HONEY AND MUSTARD *serves 2*

1 tbsp runny honey
1 tbsp wholegrain mustard
2 duck breasts halves, skinned
2 heads bok choi, trimmed and ribboned
oil for roasting and frying
½ cup wholegrain brown rice, cooked

Preheat the oven to 190°C/375°F/gas mark 5. Mix the honey and mustard in a small bowl to form a marinade. Coat the duck breast halves with the marinade and then place them in a lightly oiled roasting pan. Pour over any remaining marinade. Cover and bake for 20 minutes or until cooked through. While the duck is cooking, stir-fry the bok choi in a little oil. When the duck is ready, leave it to sit for a few minutes before serving with the freshly cooked rice and bok choi.

078

chicken

This hugely versatile and popular meat has a host of health-boosting properties.

Chicken is a good source of the mineral selenium, an infection-fighting antioxidant often missing from the diet. It contains the anti-viral amino acid lysine, helpful for suppressing the cold-sore virus. Chicken's vitamin B3 and B6 content will help to maintain a healthy nervous system. A useful source of protein, and low fat if the skin is removed, chicken contributes to the growth and repair of all the body's cells.

NUTRIENTS Vitamins B3, B6; potassium, selenium; lysine; protein

ZESTY CHICKEN CASSEROLE *serves 4*

3 tbsp olive oil
2 onions, sliced
8 skinless chicken thighs
1 tbsp all-purpose flour, seasoned
1¼ cups vegetable bouillon
grated zest of 1 orange
juice of 2 oranges
⅔ cup white wine
5 portobello mushrooms, sliced

Heat 2 tbsp of olive oil in a skillet, add the onions and fry for 10 minutes. Transfer to a plate. Toss the chicken in the flour, heat the remaining oil, add the chicken and fry until browned. Add the bouillon, onions, orange juice and zest, and white wine. Bring to a boil, reduce the heat, cover, and simmer for 25 minutes, then stir in the mushrooms and cook for 5 minutes. Serve with rice.

○ ⊙ ✋ ♡

fresh tuna

NUTRIENTS Vitamins B3, B6, B12, D, E; iodine, selenium; omega-3 fatty acids

A member of the mackerel family, tuna is rich in healthy oils and immunity-boosting minerals.

Tuna contains vitamin E and selenium, which are needed for the production of disease-fighting antibodies, and many B-vitamins, which enhance energy. Like other oily fish, it has high levels of omega-3 fatty acids, a family of essential fatty acids that can help to prevent heart disease, cancer and depression. Omega-3s also play a role in balancing the immune system, helping to reduce allergic reactions. They are also anti-inflammatory, calming conditions such as rheumatoid arthritis and eczema.

Always choose fresh rather than canned tuna, as the canning process destroys omega-3 fats.

TUNA NIÇOISE *serves 4*

juice of 1 lemon
½ tsp salt
1 tsp Dijon mustard
5 tbsp olive oil
pinch of black pepper
4 tuna steaks
4 medium potatoes, cooked and
   sliced

¼ lb green beans
4 handfuls mixed salad leaves
4 tomatoes, cut into segments
handful black olives

Whisk together the lemon juice, salt, mustard, olive oil and black pepper. Place the tuna steaks on

a large plate and coat in the vinaigrette mixture. Chill for 1 hour, then broil for 4–6 minutes. Combine all the vegetables in a large salad bowl and drizzle over remaining vinaigrette. Top with the tuna steaks, and serve.

○ ⓒ ✿ ○ ♥

salmon

Salmon is high in healthy oils, which are crucial to a healthy immune system.

Salmon is an excellent source of omega-3 fatty acids. They regulate the activity of white blood cells and exhibit anti-inflammatory properties. They also help to control cholesterol and fat levels – protecting the cardiovascular system and reducing the risk of heart disease and other circulatory problems. Salmon is rich in many antioxidants, including vitamin A – which helps to keep the blood and nervous systems healthy; vitamin D, which aids calcium absorption and is good for general bone health; and selenium – a powerful antioxidant mineral which also helps to produce antibodies.

Buy wild or organic farmed salmon in order to maximize the benefits from eating this tasty fish.

NUTRIENTS Vitamins A, B12, D, folate; selenium; omega-3 fatty acids

SALMON FISHCAKES
serves 2

2 small salmon fillets, skinless and boneless
4 small potatoes, peeled and chopped
2 tbsp olive oil
1 onion, finely chopped
1 egg, beaten
a handful of fresh parsley, chopped

Bake or steam the salmon for 20 minutes until cooked through. Boil and lightly mash the potatoes. Sauté the onion in 1 tbsp of oil until soft. Mix all the ingredients (except the oil) and form into 8 small fishcakes. Chill for 1 hour. Gently fry the fishcakes in the remaining oil until crisp on both sides. Serve.

C ✋ ⊙ ♥

mackerel

NUTRIENTS Vitamins B3, B6, B12, D; iodine, potassium, selenium; omega-3 fatty acids

One of the best fish choices for overall health, mackerel is packed with nutrients.

> One serving a week of an oily fish, such as mackerel, can help to prevent heart disease.

Mackerel is an excellent source of omega-3 fatty acids, which help to keep cholesterol levels low and, studies suggest, could also be effective in preventing cancer and depression. Omega-3 fats are also important for healthy joints and skin. Mackerel contains vitamin B6, which the body needs in order to make key amino acids for immune health, and it is one of the few food sources of vitamin D, which is crucial for good bone development. In addition, mackerel is rich in selenium, an antioxidant mineral which is vital for immune function.

SEARED MACKEREL AND FENNEL SALAD *serves 4*

2 bulbs Florence fennel, sliced
1 tbsp olive oil
4 cloves garlic
4 oranges, peeled and sliced
4 fresh mackerel, filleted

Preheat the oven to 200°C/400°F/gas mark 6. Place the fennel and garlic on a baking sheet, drizzle with olive oil and roast for 15 minutes. Add the orange slices and roast for a further 5 minutes. In a skillet, fry the mackerel in the remaining olive oil for 5 minutes. Add the roasted ingredients, toss together for 2 minutes, then serve.

fresh anchovy

This small, slender oily fish is a good source of protein and omega-3 fatty acids.

NUTRIENTS Vitamins B2, B3, D; calcium, iron, phosphorous; omega-3 fatty acids; protein

Fresh anchovy is rich in omega-3 fatty acids, which the body converts to prostaglandins, substances essential for immune function, reducing inflammation, controlling levels of cholesterol and boosting mood. It is one of the best sources of vitamin D, which we need to moderate the immune system by reducing its activity when necessary, and is also vital for healthy bones. Anchovy also contains protein and B-vitamins – both needed for energy production.

Anchovy is rich in iron, which is crucial for healthy blood and circulation.

ANCHOVY OPEN SANDWICHES *serves 4*

4 slices rye bread
1 clove garlic, crushed
2 tbsp olive oil
kosher salt and black pepper, to serve
3 cups cherry tomatoes, sliced
2-oz can anchovy fillets in olive oil, drained

Lightly broil the rye bread on both sides. Meanwhile, mix the garlic into the olive oil in a cup, and brush the mixture over the toast, when ready. Top with the tomatoes and anchovies, season, and serve.

shrimp

NUTRIENTS Vitamins B3, B12; calcium, iodine, magnesium, phosphorous, potassium, selenium, zinc; protein

The world's most popular crustaceans, shrimp are rich in immunity-boosting nutrients.

Shrimp contain high levels of immune-essential minerals, including zinc, which we need to produce the enzymes that keep cancer at bay, and to help develop other disease-fighting cells. These shellfish also contain selenium, a potent antioxidant mineral which helps in the production of antibodies, and improves the efficiency of white blood cells at recognizing unwanted invaders. Shrimp are a good source of protein, which is necessary for building healthy tissues and boosting energy.

SHRIMPS WITH BELL PEPPER SAUCE *serves 4*

4 red bell peppers, cored and chopped
1 tomato, chopped
2 cloves garlic, crushed
2 tbsp fresh parsley, chopped
1 tbsp white wine vinegar
1¾ lb cooked shrimp
1 Iceberg lettuce

Place the bell peppers on a baking sheet in the oven and bake for 10 minutes until soft. Mix together in a bowl with the tomato, garlic, parsley, and vinegar. Shred the lettuce and divide among 4 bowls. Peel the shrimp and place a few in each bowl, before topping with the bell pepper mixture.

oyster

Love them or loathe them, oysters are packed full of minerals.

Oysters contain high levels of two immune essentials: zinc and selenium. It is these minerals that give oysters their reputation as an aphrodisiac, as zinc in particular is vital for healthy reproductive organs as well as building resistance to colds and other illnesses. These shellfish contain vitamin E and omega-3 fatty acids for heart health, and contain brain-boosting B-vitamins. Oysters are also a source of vitamin D, needed for healthy bones and teeth.

It takes at least three years to grow an oyster, and up to seven to produce the giant "royals".

NUTRIENTS Vitamins B3, B12, D; calcium, magnesium, selenium, zinc; omega-3 fatty acids

TOASTED OYSTERS
serves 4

16 oysters
4 tbsp oatmeal
freshly ground black pepper
½ stick butter
juice of 1 lemon

Remove the oysters from their shells and spread them out on kitchen paper so that the excess liquid runs off. Place the oatmeal on a plate and season with pepper, then roll the oysters in the mixture until they are coated lightly. Melt the butter in a skillet and fry the oysters for 2 minutes, then drizzle with a little lemon juice, and serve.

NUTRIENTS Vitamins B2, B12; calcium, magnesium, phosphorus, potassium; bacteria cultures

bio-yoghurt

Also known as live or probiotic yoghurt, bio-yoghurt is an immune-system savior.

Always choose plain yoghurt as flavoured varieties are often high in sugar or artificial sweeteners.

Bio-yoghurt contains health-boosting lactobacillus and bifida bacteria. A healthy gut should be teeming with these, but stress, antibiotics, and poor diet can allow "unfriendly" bacteria to take over. Eating one pot of live yoghurt a day can help redress the balance, helping the body to fight off infections, as well as allowing the gut to absorb other essential immunity-boosting nutrients efficiently. Yoghurt also stimulates the production of anti-viral agents, which enhance immune response and help prevent cancer. It's an excellent source of calcium, and those who are intolerant to milk often find yoghurt acceptable.

SEEDY APPLE YOGHURT *serves 1*

1 green apple, cored and deseeded
2 tbsp sunflower seeds
⅔ cup plain bio-yoghurt

Chop the apple into bite-sized chunks and place in a small bowl. Spoon the yoghurt over it, then sprinkle on the seeds. and eat immediately. Can be enjoyed as a breakfast or as a snack at any time of the day.

086

peppermint

This dark green, strongly-flavored variety of mint can help beat colds and 'flu.

NUTRIENTS Vitamins B2, B3, C, E, beta-carotene, folate; calcium, iron, magnesium; volatile oils

Peppermint contains menthol, a volatile oil useful for clearing congestion from colds and chest infections. It also promotes the secretion of digestive juices, making peppermint a helpful indigestion remedy. It is calming and anti-inflammatory, and also a good source of the minerals iron, needed for healthy blood, and calcium, for strong bones and teeth.

PIPERADE *serves 1*

1 yellow bell pepper, cored, deseeded and sliced
1 onion, sliced
3 tbsp olive oil
2 medium tomatoes, sliced
a pinch of cayenne pepper
1 tbsp fresh mint, finely chopped
1 egg

Fry the bell pepper and onion in the oil over a low heat until the onion is soft and golden. Add the tomatoes, cayenne pepper and mint. Stir for 2 minutes, then break the egg over the vegetables and cook until the yolk is cooked as desired. Serve immediately.

Menthol can help to purify the breath, so chew a mint leaf after eating pungent foods.

chamomile

NUTRIENTS Flavonoids, tannins, coumarins, valerianic acid

Thought to calm the nerves, this medicinal plant is one of the most widely-used healing herbs.

Chamomile contains antioxidant flavonoids which help to fight harmful free radicals and protect against infection and disease. One of these flavonoids, quercetin, has powerful anti-inflammatory properties, and is useful for soothing the digestive tract. Chamomile is a mild sedative, and when taken as a tea can aid sleep and calm nerves, allowing the immune system to function efficiently.

BEDTIME TEA
makes 1 cup

**2 tsp dried chamomile
1 tsp valerian
1 tsp passion flower leaves
manuka honey, to taste**

Warm a teapot. Mix the herbs together and place in the teapot. Pour in 1 cup boiling water. Infuse for 10 minutes, then strain and pour into mug, adding honey to taste.

Cooled chamomile tea bags are soothing for sore or infected eyes.

○ ◐ ◓ ◉

echinacea

This herb is the most important immune stimulant.

Renowned for its ability to fight colds and other illnesses, echinacea's active ingredients include echinacin, a substance that helps to prevent disease-causing microbes from invading cells. The herb also contains glycosides called echinacosides, which act as natural antibiotics. As well as helping to prevent colds, 'flu, and other infections, echinacea is anti-fungal and can stimulate immune response and ease allergic reactions.

NUTRIENTS Echinacin, glycosides, volatile oils

ECHINACEA AND NETTLE TEA *serves 1*

2 tsp chopped nettles
1 tsp dried echinacea
1 tsp dried cleavers
1 tsp dried thyme
1 tsp dried borage
1 tsp dried liquorice

Mix the nettles and herbs together, then place in a warmed teapot, pour on boiling water and let infuse for 10 minutes before drinking.

Use echinacea in the winter to boost your resistance to disease.

thyme

NUTRIENTS Beta-carotene; calcium, magnesium, manganese; flavonoids; volatile oils

This Mediterranean herb has a heady scent and a wealth of disease-fighting properties.

Thyme contains high levels of thymol, a powerfully antiseptic oil helpful for beating infections of the respiratory tract, including bronchitis, laryngitis and whooping cough, as well as easing the symptoms of asthma. The oil is also anti-spasmodic, making it useful for soothing bloating and irritable bowel symptoms. It has potent antifungal effects and can help fight candida as well as being helpful used topically in a compress for fungal skin conditions.

THYME CHICKEN *serves 4*

4 skinless and boneless chicken breasts halves
8 sprigs of fresh thyme
1 lemon, cut into quarters
1 tbsp olive oil

Preheat the oven to 200°C/400°F/gas mark 5. Cut a slit in each of the chicken portions, and stuff each one with 2 sprigs of thyme and 1 slice of lemon. Place on a baking sheet and drizzle over the oil, then bake for 30 minutes. Serve with rice or potatoes.

Thyme is a versatile herb that can be drunk as a tea or added to cooking.

elderflower

The flowering top of the elder plant is a traditional remedy for coughs, colds, and hayfever.

Elderflower is rich in circulation-boosting flavonoids, including rutin which helps to tone the capillaries. It also contains choline, a member of the B-vitamin family which is thought to improve brain function, and glycosides, which have potent medicinal actions. Elderflower can help to promote sweating, encouraging detoxification, and it boosts overall resistance to illness. It is also useful for treating gout and calming allergic responses.

Elderflower contains substances which help to reduce catarrh.

NUTRIENTS Vitamin C, flavonoids; choline; glycosides; omega-3 and -6 fatty acids (trace); pectin; tannins; volatile oils

ELDERFLOWER REFRESHER *serves 1*

½ cup boiling water
1 tsp honey
1 head of fresh elderflowers
1 slice lime
ice cubes, to serve

In a bowl, pour the water and honey onto the elderflowers and lime. Cover and let infuse until cooled, then strain and pour into a glass. Serve with ice cubes.

rosemary

NUTRIENTS Beta-carotene; calcium, iron, magnesium; saponins; flavonoids, volatile oils

This wonderfully fragrant and intensely-flavored herb has a range of health-enhancing properties.

A pungent herb, rosemary is known for its circulation-boosting abilities. It contains flavonoids, important for strengthening blood capillaries. Rosemary is also a tonic for the heart and digestive system, and is rich in bioactive oils that have an anti-microbial effect, making it useful in fighting colds. It contains minerals which help to fortify the immune system, including iron and it has high levels of saponins, plant compounds which have detoxifying abilities.

SOOTHING ROSEMARY TEA *serves 1*

1 tsp dried rosemary
1 tsp dried marjoram
1 tsp dried feverfew
1 tsp dried peppermint

Mix the herbs well and place in a teapot. Add one cup of boiling water, and let infuse for 10 minutes, then strain and drink.

sage

Musty in flavor with a potent aroma, sage is a traditional herbal remedy.

Sage is anti-bacterial and anti-mucosal so it is useful for beating colds as it helps to clear catarrh as well as fight off germs. Its antiseptic properties make it excellent for healing gum problems and sore throats when drunk as a tea or used as a gargle. A sage infusion taken after eating can ease indigestion and bloating, as it is an anti-spasmodic herb – put 1 teaspoonful of the dried herb into a cup and pour on cooled, boiled water. Leave for 15 minutes, then strain and drink.

NUTRIENTS Beta-carotene; calcium, magnesium; flavonoids; tannins, saponins; volatile oils

SIMPLE SAGE STUFFING
serves 4

2 onions
1 cup fresh bread crumbs
1 tsp dried sage
black pepper
2 tbsp butter, melted

Preheat the oven to 200°C/ 400°F/ gas mark 6. Quarter the onions and cook in boiling water until tender. Then drain them and chop them finely. Place in a bowl, mix in the bread crumbs, sage, and pepper, then add the melted butter to help the mixture stick together. Place scoops of it on a baking sheet dotted with butter, and bake for 15 minutes. Serve with meat and vegetables.

Sage has stimulant properties and should be avoided by pregnant women, and people with epilepsy.

green tea

NUTRIENTS Vitamin C; flavonoids

Not just a refreshingly different brew, green tea is packed with powerful healing nutrients.

Green tea comes from the same plant, *camellia sinensis*, as ordinary black tea, but has been processed differently, leaving important nutrients intact. It is grown in high areas in countries with warm, wet climates such as Japan and India, but China is the biggest tea producer. The medicinal properties of green tea have been recognized there for over 4,000 years. It has a fresh, astringent flavor.

GREEN TEA'S IMMUNITY-BOOSTING PROPERTIES

This humble hot drink is a powerhouse of polyphenols – potent antioxidant flavonoids which neutralize damaging free radicals, helping to prevent disease. Tea's polyphenols include catechins, which counteract cancer-causing agents. It is also anti-inflammatory and can prevent flare-ups of allergic conditions such as asthma. Green tea can help to lower blood pressure and cholesterol and stop the hardening of the arteries, reducing the risk of heart disease and strokes. Its anti-bacterial abilities mean it can fight tooth decay and gum disease.

USING GREEN TEA

In order to maximize the benefits of green tea, you need to drink it strong – leave it to brew for at least five minutes. However, some people find this too bitter and compromise by drinking it weaker. Green tea is available both loose and in teabags, with natural flavorings such as lemon and apple, and herbs such as digestion-soothing peppermint and brain-boosting ginkgo biloba added for further health benefits.

Choose high quality gunpowder green tea if possible, preferably organic. Green tea is best drunk without milk, but you could add lemon or honey to taste.

GREEN TEA FACTS

• Although green tea contains less caffeine than black tea, it still has stimulant effects and should be avoided close to bedtime or by those prone to anxiety.

• The ancient Greeks called tea "the divine leaf", and used it to treat respiratory complaints, such as colds and asthma.

• Green tea's ability to fight free radicals means it has powerful anti-aging properties.

MOROCCAN MINT TEA
serves 4

2 tbsp gunpowder green tea
4 cups boiling water
good bunch of fresh mint
brown sugar, to taste

Place the tea in a teapot, cover with boiling water and let steep for 3 minutes. Wash the mint, pull out a few sprigs to save for each serving, then add the rest to the pot and leave for a further 5 minutes. Pour into glasses, adding sugar if desired, and decorate with the saved sprigs of mint.

NUTRIENTS Phenols, volatile oils

ginger

Native to India and China, ginger is one of the most important spices for fighting colds and 'flu.

Versatile as both a medicinal spice and a cooking ingredient, ginger boosts the circulation and helps the body to detoxify. Its warming oils have potent antiseptic and expectorant properties, making it a useful remedy for colds and bronchial infections – try a tea made from hot water poured onto some grated fresh ginger. Studies have found that ginger can counteract nausea, and is able to ease both travel and pregnancy sickness. It also helps to soothe digestive problems.

GINGER AND TOFU STIR-FRY *serves 4*

6 cloves garlic, crushed
4-inch piece fresh ginger, grated
1 package firm tofu, diced
soy sauce
cayenne pepper, to taste
4 tbsp olive oil
1 head broccoli, cut into florets
1 green bell pepper, cored and chopped
14oz bean sprouts
1 cup flaked almonds

In a bowl place the garlic, ginger, cayenne pepper, and tofu and drizzle on enough soy sauce to cover. Marinate for 10 minutes. Heat the oil in a wok and add the tofu marinade, vegetables, and bean sprouts, and stir-fry until lightly cooked. Add the almonds, stir through, then remove from the heat, and serve.

black cumin

Also known as *nigella*, black cumin is a traditional Asian remedy for gastro-intestinal disorders.

Black cumin is a spice which has long been valued in Asia for its medicinal properties. Recent studies have suggested that it has powerful anti-microbial and anti-bacterial properties, and aids the recovery of the digestive system after food poisoning. Its essential fatty acids help to balance the immune system and to moderate allergic reactions, while its oil stimulates immune response, protecting against cancer. Black cumin also has an antimucosal effect, making it effective during colds and other infections of the respiratory tract.

NUTRIENTS Vitamins B1, B2; manganese, potassium; omega-3 and -6 fatty acids; volatile oils

SPICE TEA *serves 1*

1 tbsp black cumin seeds
1 tsp manuka honey
1 cup boiling water

Add the seeds and honey to a mug, then pour on enough boiling water to fill it, stirring continuously. Cover and leave for 10 minutes for the flavors to mingle, then drink.

Black cumin seeds have little aroma, but when rubbed in the fingers they give off a peppery smell and a spicy flavour when cooked.

960

turmeric

NUTRIENTS Vitamin B3; calcium, iron; curcumin

Often used as a cheaper alternative to saffron, this spice should be appreciated for its own virtues.

Turmeric contains curcumin, a powerful antioxidant chemical that detoxifies carcinogens and calms inflammation, making it useful for easing auto-immune conditions such as rheumatoid arthritis and allergies. Curcumin helps to prevent the build up of fatty deposits in the arteries, and so may protect against conditions including Alzheimer's and heart disease. Turmeric has also been shown to inhibit the growth of cancer cells.

FRAGRANT RICE
serves 4

2 cups basmati rice
3 tbsp pine nuts
3 tbsp olive oil
2 large onions, finely chopped
3 tbsp raisins
½ tsp turmeric

Soak the rice for 1 hour, then drain. Gently toast the pine nuts in the oil, then add the onions and sauté them until soft and golden. Add the raisins, rice and turmeric, stir, then add enough water to cover. Bring to a boil, reduce the heat and simmer until the water is absorbed. Continue to add a little more water at a time, simmering until the rice is cooked, about 20 minutes. Serve immediately.

horseradish

This close relative of mustard can help to fight infection and boost circulation.

Horseradish has antispasmodic properties, promotes the flow of bile and is particularly good for sinus problems. It is a powerful circulatory stimulant, and also boosts digestion. Its anti-bacterial properties make it a useful cold remedy, while the volatile mustard oil it contains gives it expectorant capabilities, beneficial for loosening catarrh. Its vitamin C content is useful for generally bolstering the immune response.

NUTRIENTS Vitamin C; calcium, magnesium, phosphorous; volatile oils

Avoid horseradish if you have an underactive thyroid.

APPLE AND HORSERADISH SAUCE *makes 1 small bowl*

2 large tart apples, peeled, cored and grated
2 tbps freshly grated horseradish
juice of 1 lemon
1 tsp salt
2 tsp fresh mint, finely chopped

1 cup soured cream or fromage frais

Combine all the ingredients together in a bowl and mix thoroughly. Chill for 1 hour, then serve as an accompaniment to a meat or vegetable dish.

garlic

NUTRIENTS Vitamin B6; iron, magnesium, phosphorous, selenium, zinc; amino acids, volatile oils

An ingredient few cooks would be without, this pungent bulb has many therapeutic properties.

Widely used in cooking throughout the world, garlic is thought to have originated in central Asia. It was used in ancient Egypt and Greece, where it played a role in rituals as well as being an important medicinal food. Traditionally garlic was used to fight a range of diseases, from gastro-intestinal conditions to respiratory infections.

GARLIC'S IMMUNITY-BOOSTING PROPERTIES

Garlic is a potent anti-microbial, boosting the production of white blood cells and fighting off bacteria, parasites, fungi, and viruses. These properties make it a useful weapon against conditions from yeast infections to food poisoning and the common cold. Garlic helps boost heart health by actively lowering cholesterol levels, and allicin, a volatile oil found in the bulb, may help suppress the formation of tumors. It is also a powerful antioxidant, thanks to its amino acids, helping it to enhance overall immune function.

USING GARLIC

Versatile and tasty, garlic can be added to virtually any savory dish to boost its flavor – add one clove per person for its full health-boosting effects. It gives a kick to stir-fries, casseroles, and sauces, and can be chopped and added raw to salads and dressings. Garlic can also be taken in supplement form.

GARLIC FACTS

• Be careful not to eat an excess of garlic if you are taking medication to combat high blood pressure, as garlic can exaggerate the effects of the drugs.

• Fresh parsley can help to eradicate the strong smell of garlic on the breath.

• Garlic's sulfur compounds can irritate gastric ulcers.

• Garlic bulbs keep best stored in a cool, dry place. If the air is too damp they tend to sprout, and if it is too warm the cloves eventually turn to grey powder.

TOMATO, BASIL AND GARLIC SALAD *serves 4*

1¾ lb large ripe
  tomatoes, sliced
4 tbsp fresh basil, roughly
  chopped
2 garlic cloves, finely chopped
6 tbsp olive oil
2 tbsp balsamic vinegar
kosher salt and pepper to taste

Arrange the tomatoes flat on a large plate, and sprinkle over the remaining ingredients. Serve immediately.

mustard seed

NUTRIENTS Vitamins B1, B2, B3, carotenoids; calcium, iron, magnesium, zinc; volatile oils

The Latin name *mustum ardens* literally means "burning paste" – it's not hard to understand why!

Mustard seed's potent volatile oils make it useful for helping to fight off colds. It stimulates the circulation and encourages sweating, helping to expel toxins. Mustard seed also contains small amounts of immunity-boosting minerals, including blood-enhancing iron and antioxidant zinc, as well as B-vitamins, which can increase energy.

Mustard seed can be an irritant if used excessively, so always use it sparingly.

MASALA CHICKEN

serves 4

2 tbsp ghee
2 onions, sliced
2 tsp fresh ginger, grated
2 cloves garlic, crushed
1 tsp black mustard seeds
1 red chili, deseeded and chopped finely
2 tsp garam masala
2 tsp ground cumin
4 chicken breast halves
1 cup water
½ cup coconut milk
1 tbsp fresh cilantro, chopped

Heat the ghee in a wok and stir-fry the onions, ginger and garlic in it for 2 minutes. Add the seeds, chili, and spices, and stir-fry for a further 3 minutes. Then add the chicken and water and simmer, uncovered, until the water has evaporated and the chicken is tender. Add the coconut milk and cilantro, stir until heated through and serve.

cayenne pepper

This fiery spice is actually a finely ground variety of chili and has the same properties.

Cayenne is a circulatory stimulant, helping to dilate blood vessels and increase blood supply to all parts of the body. This makes it useful for those experiencing general debility and malaise, such as post viral fatigue (ME) sufferers. It is also powerfully anti-bacterial, can break down catarrh and has antioxidant properties which aid the body in fighting the damage caused by free radicals.

NUTRIENTS Vitamin B3, carotenoids; calcium, iron, magnesium; flavonoids; volatile oils

People suffering from gastritis, stomach ulcers, or high blood pressure should avoid cayenne pepper.

SPICY CHICKEN *serves 4*

1 tsp cayenne pepper
1 tsp chopped chilies
juice and zest of 1 lime
1 tbsp honey
1 tbsp dried oregano
1 tbsp dried basil
4 chicken breast halves
½ cup soured cream,
   to serve

In a bowl blend together the cayenne pepper, chilies, lime, honey, and herbs. Coat the chicken breasts in the marinade and let marinate for 2 hours. Cook under a medium broiler for about 30 minutes. Serve with the soured cream.

ailment directory

ACNE

The medical term for spots, acne is common in teenagers but can also affect adults. Cut out sugar and increase fiber intake in the form of fresh fruits and vegetables to improve digestive health and promote clearer skin. Zinc and vitamins B, C, and E are also helpful.

Foods to eat

avocado (p.24); bio-yoghurt (p.102); Brazil nut (p.66); evening primrose oil (p.73); nettle (p.30); oats (p.76); salmon (p.97); spinach (p.26); watercress (p.31)

ARTHRITIS (RHEUMATOID)

Rheumatoid arthritis is an inflammatory condition, so avoid foods that contribute to inflammation, such as sugar, refined carbohydrates, citrus fruits, and alcohol. Instead, follow a diet high in anti-oxidant fruit and vegetables, and include nuts, seeds, and, oily fish in your diet to maintain healthy joints.

Foods to eat

beet (p.16); broccoli (p.36); mackerel (p.98); oats (p.76); onion (p.14); papaya (p.41); pineapple (p.40); sesame seed and oil (p.74)

ASTHMA

Identifying and avoiding food allergens (such as milk, wheat, nuts and, fish), and limiting fat and sugar intake can help to control this respiratory illness.

Foods to eat

black cumin (p.113); broccoli (p.35); carrot (p.11); cayenne pepper (p.119); garlic (pp.116–17); green tea (p.110); horseradish (p.115); nettle (p.30); papaya (p.41); red bell pepper (p.15); shiitake (pp.20–21); sweet potato (p.10)

BRONCHITIS

Inflammation of the lining of the bronchial tubes, bronchitis is caused by a virus. Eat foods with anti-viral and expectorant properties.

Foods to eat

aduki bean (p.75), curly kale (p.34); elderflower (p.107); garlic (p.116-7); onion (p.14); rosemary (p.108); thyme (p.106)

CANCER

A diet high in fresh fruits and vegetables may help to prevent cancer. To treat the disease itself, choose cleansing, nutrient-dense foods containing phytochemicals that fight tumor growth.

Foods to eat

broccoli (p.36); Brussels sprouts (p.29); cherry (p.58); garbanzo (p.86); grapefruit (pp.52–3); green tea (pp.110–1); Savoy cabbage (p.36); shiitake (pp.20–1)

CANDIDIASIS

This is a infection is caused by the yeast *candida albicans*. Drugs (particularly antibiotics, immuno-suppressants and, steroids), stress and, poor diet can all promote an overgrowth of candida (thrush). There are two forms of thrush – oral and vaginal. Oral thrush produces thin, white, moist, plaques inside the mouth, which rub off to leave red, sore patches. It mainly affects sick babies, the immuno-compromised and the elderly. Vaginal thrush causes abnormal vaginal discharge, irritation and soreness.

Foods to Eat

bio-yoghurt (p.102); black cumin (p.113); garlic (pp.116–7); thyme (p.106)

COMMON COLD

Help your body to fight common cold viruses by avoiding dairy products and by eating lots of fruit and vegetables rich in vitamin C and the mineral zinc.

Foods to eat

black cumin (p.113); blueberry (pp.56–7); garlic (pp.116–7); ginger (p.112); lemon (p.50); oats (p.76); onion (p.14); orange (p.51); rosemary (p.108); thyme (p.106)

CYSTITIS

This condition, which is a bacterial infection of the urinary tract, can be helped by eating plenty of fresh foods rich in vitamins A and C, and, the mineral zinc. Avoid excess sugar, caffeine, alcohol and, foods containing additives and drink plenty of water to keep well hydrated.

Foods to eat

aduki bean (p.75); asparagus (p.27); bio-yoghurt (p.102); Brussels sprouts (p.29); cherry (p.58); cranberry (p.60); garlic (pp.116–7); guava (p.43); sesame seed and oil (p.74)

DEPRESSION (MILD)

Characterized by tearfulness, anxiety and, feelings of hopelessness, depression affects one in four people at some stage in life. Beat it by cutting out alcohol, cigarettes and, sugary food, exercising, and choosing foods high in omega 3-fatty acids and B-vitamins.

Foods to eat

mackerel (p.98); oats (p.76); quinoa (p.79); rice (p.80); salmon (p.97); spinach (p.26); tuna (p.96)

ECZEMA

Limit the frequency of outbreaks of this common skin condition by first identifying and avoiding the foods you are sensitive to. Take steps to reduce your intake of dairy and processed foods and follow a diet that is rich in essential fats, vitamin A and, zinc.

Foods to eat

chamomile (p.104); carrot (p.11); curly kale (pp.34–5); echinacea (p.105); evening primrose oil (p.73); pine nut (p.65); pumpkin seed (p.71); walnut (p.63)

FUNGAL INFECTIONS

Common fungal infections include thrush (see *Candidiasis*) and athlete's foot. Help your body to fight them by avoiding alcohol, dairy and, refined sugar products and by limiting yeast consumption (including bread and yeast extract).

Foods to eat

Brazil nut (p.66); chamomile (p.104); carrot (p.11); garlic (pp.116–7); ginger (p.112); grapefruit (pp.52–3); rice (p.80)

FOOD POISONING

Caused by bacteria such as *e.coli* and *listeria*, food poisoning can cause vomiting, diarrhoea and, fever. To aid recovery, drink lots of water, choose detoxifying foods and restore your body's natural balance by eating foods that encourage the growth of friendly bacteria.

Foods to eat

aduki bean (p.75); asparagus (p.27); bio-yoghurt (p.102); globe artichoke (p.28); grapes (p.47); green tea (pp.110–1); oats (p.76); rhubarb (p.19)

HAY FEVER

A diet rich in immunity-boosting nutrients such as vitamin E, beta-carotene, selenium and, magnesium can help to calm symptoms of this

allergic condition, which include a runny nose, sneezing and, itchy eyes. Avoid wheat and dairy products, drink plenty of fluids and eat foods containing vitamin C, a natural anti-histamine.

Foods to eat

avocado (pp.24–5); beet (pp.16–7); green tea (pp.110-1); guava (p.43); papaya (p.41); shiitake (pp.20–21); spinach (p.26)

HEART DISEASE

One of the causes of heart disease is the blockage of arteries by cholesterol and waste matter, heart disease is a big killer in the Western world. Avoid saturated fats (found in red meat, cheese and, processed foods), use healthy oils and eat high-fibre foods.

Foods to eat

almond (p.69); avocado (pp.24–25); blueberry (pp.56-7); garlic (p.116); grapefruit (pp.52–3); mackerel (p.98); oats (p.76); salmon (p.97)

HERPES SIMPLEX

The virus that causes cold sores thrives on the amino acid arginine, found in chocolate and nuts, so avoid these foods. Instead, eat foods rich in anti-viral vitamin C and, beta-carotene. During an attack foods rich in vitamin C and zinc can speed up the healing process.

Foods to eat

echinacea (p.105); garlic (pp.116–7); guava (p.43); kiwi fruit (p.39); pumpkin seed (p.71); shiitake (pp.20 –1); spinach (p.26); tomato (p.18)

HIV AND AIDS

A virus transmitted by body fluids, AIDS and its precursor, HIV, are a growing problem throughout the world. If affected eat plenty of fresh, preferably organic whole foods, and choose foods rich in zinc and vitamin C, as well as superfoods such as shiitake and green tea.

Foods to eat

beet (pp.16–17); Brazil nut (pp.66-7); broccoli (p.36); grapefruit (pp.52–3); green tea (p.87); nettle (p.30); sweet potato (p.10); shiitake (pp.20–1)

INFLUENZA ('FLU)

Maintaining a healthy immune system is the best way to combat this viral infection with its severe cold-like symptoms. If affected eat a diet rich in

antioxidant vitamins and minerals and drink plenty of fluids, especially water.

Foods to Eat

See those listed for Common Cold

INFLAMMATORY BOWEL DISEASE

IBD can result in abdominal pain, bloody diarrhoea, weight loss and, poor nutrient absorption. Avoid sugar, refined carbohydrates, wheat and, dairy, and choose anti-inflammatory foods rich in vitamin C.

Foods to eat

avocado (pp.24–5); bio–yoghurt (p.102); lentil (p.85); oats (p.76); rice (p.80); soy bean (pp.88–9); spinach (p.26); walnut (p.63)

MIGRAINE

Help to lessen the frequency of these severe headaches by identifying and avoiding potential food allergens (such as cheese, coffee, chocolate and, red wine).

POST-VIRAL FATIGUE (ME)

Although the specific cause is unknown, this is a chronic condition characterized by low energy levels and, poor concentration. Post-viral fatigue often follows on from a viral illness so focusing on immune-enhancing foods can help alleviate the symptoms.

Foods to Eat

apricot (p.42), beet (pp.16–7), carrot (p.11), cherry (p.58), grape (p.47); peppermint (p.103), thyme (p.106)

SINUSITIS

This inflammation of the cavities in the bones around the nose causes headache, facial pain and a blocked nose. It is most often a complication of colds and 'flu, and may also be caused by allergy, injury or tooth infection.

Foods to Eat

See those listed for Common Cold

SORE THROAT

Throat infections can be viral or bacterial, and causes fever, malaise and, difficulty swallowing, owing to inflammation of the tonsils and/or adenoids.

Foods to Eat

blueberry (pp.56–7); carrot (p.11); garlic (pp.116–7); lemon (p.50); nettle (p.30); onion (p.14); rosemary p.108), thyme (p.106)

glossary

VITAMINS

A and beta-carotene – vitamin A and its vegetarian precursor beta-carotene are strongly anti-viral. They are important for the production of T-cells and anti-bacterial enzymes.

B1 (thiamine) – important for good digestion, strong mucous membranes, a healthy nervous system and, energy.

B2 (riboflavin) – repairs and maintains body tissues and mucous membranes, and helps convert food into energy.

B3 (niacin) – is involved in energy production and maintains healthy skin, mucous membranes, nerves, brain and, digestive system.

B5 (pantothenic acid) – an immune-system stimulant needed for the formation of antibodies, it helps the body deal with stress and maintains healthy nerves.

B6 – helps to make key immunity amino acids; boosts the action of phagocytic cells, and is important for healthy brain function.

B12 – is needed to make DNA and transport oxygen in the blood. It detoxifies the body, and assists nerve function.

Folic acid (folate) – a B vitamin vital for reproductive health and cell division; helps maintain healthy blood cells.

Biotin – necessary for healthy skin, hair, and nails plus nerves and, bone marrow. It is also involved in energy production.

Vitamin C – anti-viral, antioxidant, detoxifying, anti-allergenic, and anti-bacterial, vitamin C is crucial to immune system function.

Vitamin D – derived chiefly from sunlight, vitamin D is needed for strong bones and teeth, and to help

deactivate the immune system once an infection has passed.

Vitamin E – helps neutralize harmful free radicals; detoxify the body, and is needed for normal antibody response.

Vitamin K – aids blood clotting and wound healing and is also needed for bone metabolism.

MINERALS

Calcium – maintains strong bones and nerves; boosts phagocytes, and T-cells to help them destroy viruses and bacteria.

Chromium – helps regulate blood sugar levels and reduce cravings. It also improves and boosts protein synthesis and reduces blood fat levels.

Copper – improves iron absorption and increases oxygen in the blood. Needed for the utilization of vitamin C in the body.

Iodine – essential for good thyroid function, thereby aiding metabolism and energy levels.

Magnesium – increases absorption of calcium; needed for metabolism and, energy production, nerve transmission and muscle function.

Manganese – is important for insulin production, is needed for the production of anti-oxidant enzymes, healthy DNA, bones and nerves and, the thyroid hormone.

Phosphorous – contains phosphorus, which forms part of protein and is necessary for health.

Potassium – important for maintaining fluid levels in the body, helps produce energy.

Selenium – maintains resistance to disease, has detoxifying, anti-inflammatory and, anti-cancer properties.

Silica – anti-inflammatory, skin healing and found in oats.

Zinc – anti-oxidant, anti-viral

mineral that boosts overall immunity, and is needed for the maturation of T-cells.

OTHERS

Allicin – volatile oil found in onions and garlic that may help suppress tumors.

Amino acids – molecular units that make up proteins.

Anthocyanins – dark purple coloured pigments, that are antioxidant and aid blood flow.

Asparagin – detoxifying amino acid found in asparagus.

Bacteria cultures – friendly bacteria found in bio-yoghurt which promote good digestion and immunity in the gut.

Beta-sitosterol – plant chemical that lowers blood cholesterol and promotes prostate health.

Bromelain – an anti inflammatory enzyme that helps digest proteins.

Capsaicin – plant chemical found

in chilies, this has a natural analgesic effect.

Carotenoids – coloured pigments found in plants, these include alpha-, beta- and, gamma-carotene that all give rise to vitamin A.

Catechins – antioxidant flavonoids that help prevent cancer and heart disease.

Choline – helps regulate metabolism of fats and boosts resistance to infection.

Coumarins – chemicals with natural blood-thinning properties, may help prevent cancer.

Curcumin – detoxifying, anti-inflammatory pigment found in the spice turmeric.

Cynarin – detoxifying, liver-supporting substance.

Ellagic acid – cancer-fighting substance found in berries.

Essential fatty acids (EFAs) – including omega-3 and omega-6